continuing professional development in education

CPD: Additional Support Needs

An introduction to ASN from Nursery to Secondary

Paul Hamill and Kathleen Clark

Series editor: Brian Boyd

Published in association with the
Times Educational Supplement Scotland

D0552163

Hodder Gibson

A MEMBER OF THE HODDER HEADLINE GROUP

Every effort has been made to trace all copyright holders, but if any have been inadvertently overlooked the Publishers will be pleased to make the necessary arrangements at the first opportunity.

Although every effort has been made to ensure that website addresses are correct at time of going to press, Hodder Gibson cannot be held responsible for the content of any website mentioned in this book. It is sometimes possible to find a relocated web page by typing in the address of the home page for a website in the URL window of your browser.

Orders: please contact Bookpoint Ltd, 130 Milton Park, Abingdon, Oxon OX14 4SB. Telephone: (44) 01235 827720. Fax: (44) 01235 400454. Lines are open 9.00–6.00, Monday to Saturday, with a 24-hour message answering service. Visit our website at www.hoddereducation.co.uk. Hodder Gibson can be contacted direct on: Tel: 0141 848 1609; Fax: 0141 889 6315; email: hoddergibson@hodder.co.uk

© Paul Hamill and Kathleen Clark 2005
First published in 2005 by
Hodder Gibson, a member of the Hodder Headline Group
2a Christie Street
Paisley PA1 1NB

Impression number   10 9 8 7 6 5 4 3 2 1
Year   2010 2009 2008 2007 2006 2005

Cover illustration by David Parkin.
Typeset by Transet Limited, Coventry, England.
Printed and bound in Great Britain by CPI Bath.

A catalogue record for this title is available from the British Library

ISBN-10: 0-340-88993-4
ISBN-13: 978-0-340-889-930

About the Authors

Paul Hamill is head of the Department of Educational Support and Guidance in the Education Faculty at the University of Strathclyde. He taught for eighteen years in Primary, Secondary and Special Schools and has extensive understanding of the field of additional support needs. He has a wealth of experience as an educational consultant, having delivered effective professional development opportunities for local authorities, schools and teachers throughout Scotland.

Kathleen Clark is a Senior Lecturer in the same department. As a former primary support for learning specialist, she amassed a wealth of practical knowledge and understanding of support systems and strategies in schools from nursery to upper primary. Her main areas of interest and research are the challenge of inclusion; dyslexia and related specific learning difficulties; early intervention and literacy development.

Foreword

The *Times Educational Supplement Scotland* is delighted to be associated with the publication of this prestigious new series of books devoted to key areas in the field of continuing professional development.

Since the newspaper's birth in 1965, we have always attempted to inform, educate, and occasionally entertain the Scottish teaching profession, as well as to encourage dialogue between all educational sectors. In recent years, our commitment to the concept of encouraging educationists to constantly reflect – and act – upon best practice has been most tangibly evident in the provision of an annual CPD supplement. This offers full and detailed examination of developments in CPD from both Scottish and international contexts, and we attempt to share best practice in a manner that is both accessible and valuable.

This series of books is another testimony of our commitment to CPD. Drawing on the experience of foremost Scottish practitioners, each book attempts to offer academic rigour with a lightness of delivery that is too often found wanting in the weightier tomes that populate many educational libraries, and which are consequently left unread, except by those approaching examinations – or job interviews.

In short, we hope that these books will be welcomed in the groves of academe; but we also believe that they deserve to be read – and acted upon – by a much wider audience: those teachers across Scotland, nursery, primary and secondary, who deliver the curriculum on a daily basis to our young people.

Neil Munro
Editor, *Times Educational Supplement Scotland*

Contents

1 Additional support needs: an evolving concept

> ❛ Minds are like parachutes: they only function when open. ❜
>
> **Thomas R. Dewar**

Introduction

Since the publication of the Warnock Report in 1978 the label 'special educational need' has been widely used within Scottish education, and until fairly recently this label was perceived as conveying a more positive image than that of handicap of young people who for a variety of reasons have experienced some difficulty in learning.

In 1994 the Scottish Office Education Department (SOED) published the report 'Effective Provision for Special Educational Needs', which defined the concept of special educational needs in terms of the barriers to learning experienced by a diverse group of young people. Emphasis was placed upon the need for all teachers to share a common understanding of this complex concept, which was seen to underpin effective practice, and the report became a blueprint for all schools and policy makers in relation to supporting young people deemed to have special educational needs.

However, in 2003 the Scottish Executive Education Department (SEED) report 'Moving Forward! Additional Support for Learning' questioned the philosophy which had up until this time underpinned special needs policy and practice. For the first time the label 'special educational need' was challenged as having 'negative connotations which placed too much emphasis on weakness and problems' (p. 11) and was replaced by a new label 'additional support needs'. This represents a fairly radical change in thinking and once again demonstrates how we move forward as our depth of understanding develops within an evolving social and cultural context. Policy makers in education have always been keen to win the hearts and minds of teachers, and over the years they have introduced new terminology aimed at achieving this purpose. This was certainly the approach in relation to special educational needs, but there is evidence to suggest that instead of winning hearts and minds the result has been a rise in levels of confusion and uncertainty. In order to make sense of this situation teachers need to start at the beginning and explore the nature and range of historical factors which to a large extent have set the context for the ensuing confusion.

The deficit model

In Scotland it has for some time now been widely accepted that labels such as 'mentally handicapped', 'profoundly retarded', and 'educationally subnormal' are discriminatory and devalue individuals. However, this was not always the case and throughout the nineteenth and for most of the twentieth century the medical model prevailed, with its emphasis on categorisation and segregation. By the early nineteenth century the term 'mentally defective' had come into common usage and in 1862 the Lunacy (Scotland) Act set up charitable institutions for the care and training of imbecile children. This deficit philosophy underpinned policy and provision for the next hundred years (Thomson 1983).

In 1872 the Education (Scotland) Act emerged within the context of the Industrial Revolution with its need for a disciplined workforce. This act outlined the provision of compulsory education for all, but in practice, as attempts were made to implement this principle, it emerged that many individuals could not access effectively what was on offer because of difficulties in learning. It was not until 1907 with the Education of Defective Children (Scotland) Act that school boards were entitled to set up special schools and classes.

Unfortunately the ensuing world wars halted any further developments in the system until 1945 when the Education (Scotland) Act heralded what appeared to be a new era when for the first time all children were seen to have a basic right to education (Pearson and Lindsay 1986). In reality this act did not break new ground as it still relied heavily on the medical model with its strong focus on selection, segregation and the provision of training as opposed to education. This act simply presented a new three-tier approach based on the concepts of educable, trainable and untrainable. As Dockrell, Dunn & Milne (1978, p. 3) state 'few seemed alive to the fact that to describe human beings as ineducable and untrainable was to place them in the evolutionary scale lower than sea-lions or performing seals'. Those educationalists who put forward this new tiered system did so for what they considered to be laudable reasons and for the good of those involved. In retrospect, however, one can see clearly that they were oblivious to the potential damage inherent in such a system.

This system of categorisation was further expanded in 1954 when the Special Education Treatment (Scotland) Regulations identified nine categories of handicap: deaf, partially deaf, blind, partially sighted, mentally handicapped, epileptic, having speech defects, maladjusted, and physically handicapped. This reinforced 'the process of labelling which encouraged the creation of stereotypes that are to the disadvantage of those involved' (Ainscow 1991, p. 2). Finally in the Scottish context the Melville Committee Report (1973) was another benchmark and its basic recommendation that all children are educable and should be educated within the education system was enshrined in the Education (Scotland) Act (1974). Although the situation was beginning to change by the early 1970s the main focus was still on negative labelling and segregation based firmly on a deficit philosophy.

From handicap to need

In 1974 the Warnock Committee began the first comprehensive examination of educational provision and practice for children and young people who were still at this time being labelled as handicapped. The committee introduced the concept of need as opposed to focusing on the traditional concept of handicap, and for the first time these young people were referred to as having special educational needs. The emphasis was placed upon a young person's individual need as distinct from his/her disability. Thus the Warnock Report reflected 'both the gradual disenchantment with statutory categories and the developing rhetoric of integration' (Gilbert and Hart 1990, p. 18).

At the same time Warnock redefined the nature and purpose of assessment, indicating that the aim was no longer to place individuals into categories but to obtain a more comprehensive view of their strengths and weaknesses. The main purpose of assessment was recognised as providing guidance in relation to the most appropriate educational provision based on need. The committee suggested that a system of recording the needs of the 2% of children with severe, complex or long-term disabilities be set up. It was recommended that a Record of Needs be opened for this group of young people. This document outlined the individual's difficulties and strengths and set out what additional support was needed. It also indicated how the education authority proposed to provide support. The 2% of young people with recorded needs was a subset of a larger group of 20% who were now recognised as having special educational needs. A single concept of special educational need was introduced to include children educated in special schools and those in mainstream schools who experienced difficulty in learning and were often labelled as remedial.

At this time the vast majority of children with Records of Need were still educated in special schools, and Warnock acknowledged that there would continue to be a need for such provision. However, for the first time the idea of integration as opposed to segregation began to emerge and it was accepted that if one in five children were deemed at some time to have special educational needs it was obvious that many would have these needs identified and met in the mainstream school. In 1980 the Education (Scotland) Act enshrined in law the Warnock philosophy when it stated that children have special educational needs if they 'have greater difficulty in learning than most other children of their own age'. The philosophical objectives of the new legislation were outlined in 1996 in a study by Thomson, Stewart and Ward as follows:

- minimising the distinction within the education system between individuals with handicaps and others
- replacing the system based on statutory handicap with one that places emphasis on a profile of individual need
- increasing parental participation in the decision-making process.

Thus the Warnock report played a pivotal role in shaping future special needs policy and practice throughout the latter part of the twentieth century.

A Curriculum Model

In 1978 another key report entitled 'The Education of Pupils with Learning Difficulties in Primary and Secondary Schools in Scotland' was published in Scotland by SED. It focused exclusively on mainstream schools, and many of its recommendations echoed Warnock. In particular the HMI were not happy with the narrow definition of remedial education and suggested that it did not cover the range and diversity of learning difficulties experienced by young people in mainstream schools. They concluded that special educational needs were a whole-school responsibility and that the curriculum could be a source of learning difficulties.

These were new and fairly radical ideas which emphasised that the source of learning difficulties could reside within systems as opposed to individuals. All teachers were encouraged to rethink their educational philosophy and move away from the restrictive concept of remedial education to one of supporting the learner within the context of an appropriate curriculum. The keynote was change, and the focus was upon making the curriculum more accessible for all (Sebba, Byers and Rose 1995). Gradually the deficit model began to give way to a curricular model as a framework for understanding the concept of special educational needs and for developing the most effective systems for supporting individuals who experienced difficulty in learning. The SED (1978) report stressed throughout that 'appropriate rather than remedial education is required' (p.25) and advised that there should be much less focus on individual deficits and a greater awareness that barriers to learning could arise from a mismatch between learners and their learning environment.

This view has been consistently reinforced by research evidence since the mid 1990s (Solity 1993; Mittler 2000; Hamill and Boyd 2000, 2001). Thus the SED report of 1978 redefined and extended concepts of learning difficulties and special needs, and its recommendations had a tremendous influence on encouraging all professionals to abandon outdated practice based on remediation and replace it with the more positive context of support for learning.

This philosophy strongly influenced developing practice and provision throughout the next two decades and this was summed up by Booth and Swann (1992, p. 1) when they said that 'the resolution of difficulties in learning is now seen as the task of creating an education system that is responsive to all learners'. This was the theme taken up by the Scottish Office Education Department (SOED) in 1994 in the report 'Effective Provision for Special Educational Needs' (EPSEN) when they gave priority to ensuring that educational provision should enable all individuals to optimise their abilities and to overcome, minimise or circumvent their learning difficulties. A clear message was conveyed that meeting the needs of these young people was a central not a peripheral concern within Scottish education. The concept of special educational needs was highlighted as 'subtle and requires discussion and reflection' (p. 7) and emphasis was placed upon the need for professionals to internalise the view that an understanding of the concept of special educational need was fundamental to planning and making effective provision at all levels of the education system. The EPSEN report also clearly articulated ten distinctive features of effective provision for special educational needs:

- understanding the continuum of special needs
- effective identification and assessment procedures
- an appropriate curriculum
- forms of provision suited to needs
- effective approaches to learning and teaching
- attainment of educational goals
- parental involvement
- interprofessional cooperation
- effective management of provision
- full involvement of the young person.

By 1998 all of these recommended features were widely accepted within Scottish education and there was considerable evidence to suggest that many local authorities and schools were demonstrating good practice based on them. Therefore, in that year, SOEID, now the Scottish Executive Education Department (SEED) produced 'A Manual of Good Practice in Meeting Special Educational Needs' aimed at sharing examples of good practice and helping professionals at all levels with the development of high-quality provision across Scotland. This manual was designed to assist schools, local authorities and support services with their strategic development planning. Three key areas were covered:

- working together
- providing an appropriate curriculum
- involving young people in the decision-making process.

In relation to each of these areas, policy makers were asked to consider three questions. How are you doing? How do you know? What are you going to do now? Thus in Scotland we moved into the twenty-first century with a commitment to meeting special needs in inclusive environments where professionals were committed to a cycle of ongoing self-evaluation and where key principles are continuously reviewed, monitored and evaluated.

Moving forward – additional support needs

We have come a long way from the time when some young people were deemed to be ineducable and were denied education, and it is almost impossible now to comprehend such a negative approach. The Scottish Executive now promotes a vision of the education system that is inclusive, welcomes diversity, provides equal opportunities and develops the young person's full potential. The Standards in Scotland's Schools etc. Act (Scottish Parliament 2000) embraces the United Nation's principle established in 1989 that all children have a right to education and to have a say in decisions that affect their lives. At the same time the act confirmed the intention to create within Scottish education a presumption of mainstream inclusion and this principle is now firmly rooted within legislation. This means that wherever possible young people will be educated in mainstream schools.

Disability and anti-discrimination legislation has now been extended to education. This means that educational establishments must, by law, focus upon the rights of young people with disabilities and they have responsibilities in relation to effectively meeting their needs. The Education (Disability Strategies and Pupils' Educational Records) (Scotland) Act 2002 is of particular importance as it emphasises a commitment to effective access, communication and support, and places the onus on schools and local authorities to ensure appropriate strategies are put in place.

Once again the agenda is changing and it is recognised that some of the procedures currently in place have now outlived their usefulness and are ripe for further development. This is the case in relation to the Record of Needs which is increasingly being seen as at odds with the evolving inclusive education debate and does not sit well within the emerging legislative changes. In 2003 the Scottish Executive Education Department (SEED) set up a consultative process to determine exactly what changes were necessary to the current recording and assessment framework. This resulted in the report entitled 'Moving Forward! Additional Support for Learning' which proposed a new legislative framework replacing the label 'special educational needs' with the concept of 'additional support needs'. This change in terminology was felt to be very important as it was seen to be less stigmatising and recognised that many children will need additional support for learning at some time in their school careers. Therefore the term 'special educational needs', which had been widely used since the late 1970s, was rejected. The new legislative framework is set out in the Education (Additional Support for Learning) (Scotland) Act 2004. This is a very important development and it is worthwhile considering what the act will mean in relation to creating a system in Scotland which is more holistic, caters for diversity and supports inclusion.

Proposed changes

Since 2003 schools have been expected to provide all pupils with a Personal Learning Plan (PLP); these plans assist schools in planning effective learning opportunities for their pupils. The PLP provides a continuous record and an action plan for learning, and pupils are expected to play an active part in determining agreed learning outcomes. The majority of young people with additional support needs will not only have a PLP (which will identify their needs and can be used to ensure appropriate support is available) but also an Individual Educational Plan (IEP). The PLP will act as a co-ordinating device bringing together all current reporting and recording tools including the IEP.

It is of course still accepted that some young people face long-term complex or multiple barriers to learning and require access to additional resources and a more diverse range of specialist services. It is vitally important that the new legislation takes full account of the needs of these young people and ensures that they have access to the resources they require. This will be addressed by a Co-ordinated Support Plan (CSP), which will replace the Record of Needs and target the specific needs of young people who experience more complex learning difficulties. One of the main benefits of these proposed changes will be the focus upon a multi-agency approach in the provision of support for all young people requiring additional support, particularly those with the most complex needs. There will also be a strong focus on parental partnership with extended rights for parents of children with a CSP enabling them to challenge the level of provision proposed. Local authorities will also need to have in place a service for resolution of disputes, and an independent tribunal will be established to hear appeals.

Developments at international, national and local level have contributed to major changes in legislation, policy and practice with regards to what has been known as special educational needs and has now been redefined as additional support needs. Running parallel in recent years with these sweeping reforms is the social inclusion debate. Inclusion and inclusive education give rise to some complex issues and consequently these important topics will be addressed more fully in Chapter 2. However, it is important at the outset to set the move towards inclusion within the overall evolving context which has shaped policy and provision in relation to additional support needs.

From segregation to inclusion

In the early years of a new millennium, inclusion has become an issue which is high on the Scottish education agenda and is now one of the key priorities at all levels. At national level the UK government has clearly articulated its social inclusion policy, the Scottish Executive has incorporated this into its social justice strategy, and it is also within this social and political context that schools and local authorities have developed their own inclusive practice. Although considerable progress has been made in making 'inclusion for all' a reality, confusion and uncertainty still surround this concept. The practice of segregation is no longer accepted unquestioningly but it remains difficult to move smoothly to inclusive models that are not characterised by deficit thinking, and which do not locate the problems within individuals as opposed to systems.

In 1980 the Education (Scotland) Act took on board the thinking enshrined within the Warnock Report (DES 1978) and the SED Report (1978) when it endorsed the process of integration. A greater focus was placed on integrating into mainstream schools young people deemed to have special needs. However by the early 1990s doubts were being raised about the value of integration as a concept. There was concern that the process of integration had not been thought through as effectively as it might have been. The process tended to be driven by an ideology which was based on simply increasing the number of young people with special needs in mainstream schools without paying adequate attention to the quality of the educational experience (Slee 1996). Thus integration emerged as a strategy whereby these young people were expected to fit into an existing system; there was no recognition of the need to transform this system to accommodate the needs of these young people.

The integration process continued to be inextricably linked to the process of segregation within mainstream schools and it became clear that the concept of integration was only workable within the context of segregation. Inclusion gradually evolved as an alternative to integration, requiring schools to think about and remove environmental, structural and attitudinal barriers which underpinned exclusive practice. Inclusion implies systemic change involving radical reform at all levels of the education system. Whereas integration focused upon a group of young people traditionally labelled as having special educational needs, inclusion applies to all individuals. The focus moved away from one discrete identifiable group to the right of all young people to experience a high-quality inclusive education.

In 2003 the Scottish Executive placed an increased emphasis on inclusion by firmly establishing the promotion of inclusion and equality as one of its national priorities. This vision of inclusion 'refers to all regardless of disability, gender, sexual orientation, religious persuasion, racial origin, and cultural and linguistic background' ('Moving Forward! Additional Support for Learning' p. 22). The extent to which this vision will become reality, particularly within the education system, remains to be seen. Most schools continue to strive towards inclusion. However, theory and practice are not necessarily compatible and in Chapter 2 we will look more closely at the challenges inherent in putting inclusive principles into practice.

A teaching profession for the twenty-first century

As the concepts of special educational and additional support needs gradually evolved so too did the idea that teachers supporting these young people should have access to appropriate continuing professional development (CPD). The first training courses started in the 1920s and initially the focus was on training teachers to work with 'mentally defective' children in special schools. Thus, at the outset, teacher training reflected the deficit philosophy which prevailed at the time, and emphasis was placed on teaching aimed at remedying perceived defects residing within individuals.

By the 1950s it was common to find in most mainstream primary and secondary schools what was referred to as a group of 'backward' or 'retarded' pupils, who began to be formed into remedial classes. These young people were removed from their peer group and taught by remedial teachers. By the 1970s two parallel forms of training were provided: one focused on preparing teachers to work in special schools and the other on training mainstream remedial teachers.

One of the most sweeping changes occurred as a result of the Warnock Report and the HMI (SED) report on pupils with learning difficulties, both published in 1978. The parallel training courses were replaced by two newly validated programmes sharing common elements but still distinguished by the labels 'recorded' and 'non-recorded' signifying the group of young people being taught. This was in keeping with the existing situation whereby young people with Records of Needs were still educated almost exclusively in special schools.

These teacher training programmes continued to be delivered throughout the 1980s but by 1990 the concept of integration became dominant, and teachers working in the special needs/ mainstream support field were increasingly expected to work collaboratively across schools and across the curriculum. Thus teacher training programmes once again responded to the need for a new kind of professional who, in the mainstream schools in particular, was expected to work co-operatively with colleagues in classrooms, ensuring young people accessed an appropriate curriculum as opposed to being withdrawn for remedial treatment. A new postgraduate modular teacher training programme emerged to meet the needs of all teachers regardless of where they taught. These programmes proved to be very flexible and have successfully met the needs of teachers since 1990. They continue at this time to be widely recognised as the appropriate route for support for learning teachers who wish to develop as specialists in supporting young people with additional support needs.

It is now universally accepted that the quality of the education service in Scotland depends upon the quality of the teachers who provide it. If higher standards are to be achieved and all pupils are to be effectively supported in order to develop their full potential it is essential that all teachers are well prepared for the job they do and that they have opportunities to revitalise their skills as they move through their careers. The Chartered Teacher programme is designed to fulfil this need.

As we progress through the twenty-first century all teachers, but particularly those who wish to be designated as Chartered Teachers, will need to undertake continuing professional development that equips them to understand and effectively meet the diverse range of pupil needs which will characterise the inclusive school. To attain the Chartered Teacher Standard, teachers will have to demonstrate that they can effectively promote learning for all pupils and are able to work collaboratively with a range of colleagues. This book is designed to meet the professional development needs of these teachers but it will also be of relevance to all teachers, managers and other professionals who work with and support young people in a range of contexts.

SUMMARY

Additional support needs is a concept which has evolved over the past century and to fully understand it one must be aware of the changing philosophy which has underpinned it. Up until the 1970s the deficit model dominated thinking in relation to individuals who experienced difficulty in learning. The focus was on stereotypical images and negative labelling.

It was only in the later part of the twentieth century that professionals began to appreciate that barriers to learning all too often resided within systems rather than individuals. The term 'special educational needs' was introduced to replace the more negative labels but this term has now also come to be seen as having negative connotations. Inclusion has now emerged as the key to good practice, with the potential to transform educational systems so that all learners have access to an appropriate curriculum.

The twenty-first-century teacher is a vital part of this process and thus it is very important that he/she understands how the concept of additional support need has evolved within a historical context which has shaped and moulded current thinking.

POINTS FOR REFLECTION

1 To what extent does a deficit philosophy still underpin professional thinking and practice in relation to working with and meeting the additional support needs of some young people?

2 How can schools and teachers demonstrate that the curriculum on offer is at an appropriate level and accessible to all learners regardless of their ability?

3 Are all professionals aware that the label 'special educational needs' (SEN) is now seen to have negative connotations and has been replaced by the more positive term 'additional support needs' (ASN)?

2 Achieving inclusion in Scottish schools

> *A school should not be a preparation for life. A school should be life.*
>
> **Elbert Hubbard**

What is inclusion?

The promotion of equality of opportunity and a commitment to inclusion have traditionally been at the core of Scottish education. The most forward-thinking schools have always made every effort to take on board new initiatives and to put in place systems which aim to develop the full potential of all young people. It is however important to realise that in relation to inclusion there are no quick fixes or easy solutions. Most schools continue to strive towards full inclusion and in doing so encounter a range of complex issues which present challenges to them. There is no single route towards inclusion that will suit all schools and there is still not a universally shared understanding of what inclusion actually means. It is still open to fairly wide interpretation and debate and there is still an element of confusion surrounding terms such as inclusive schools and inclusive education. In their work on inclusive schools, Hamill and Boyd (2000, 2001, 2002) surveyed over 2000 teachers in secondary and primary schools and found that around 75% were unsure exactly what was meant by inclusion and felt that it was an initiative which was imposed upon them. It seems logical therefore to assume that if inclusion is to become a reality in schools it is a concept which must be understood and accepted by those who are expected to make it work on a day-to-day basis. We may in fact be putting the cart before the horse by trying to devise inclusive strategies without ensuring those who have to put them into practice have the opportunity to reflect on and find an answer to the question 'What is inclusion?'.

Hamill and Boyd found that the majority of teachers continued to adopt a fairly restricted view of inclusive education. When asked what they thought inclusion meant they tended to equate it with a discrete group of young people with additional support needs and many narrowed this even further to focus upon young people whose behaviour could be challenging. There was little evidence that teachers had as yet internalised the wider more diverse, dynamic definition of inclusion as a concept which reflects the environmental and social mores which impact upon educational policy and effective schooling. In their study *From Them to Us*, Booth and Ainscow (1998) emphasised the dangers inherent in adopting a narrow, restricted view of inclusive education. They provided a broad definition of inclusion which cautions professionals to avoid simply equating inclusion with special or additional support needs. Including these young people is obviously a very important aspect of inclusion but inclusion as defined by Booth and Ainscow is a much more diverse concept extending beyond special or additional support needs to include all, regardless of ability, gender, sexual orientation, religion, race and linguistic orientation.

The Standards in Scotland's Schools etc. Act (2000) reflected this inclusive philosophy and confirmed that Scottish education authorities had a duty to provide education in mainstream schools for all young people except in certain circumstances. For the first time there was a legal presumption that mainstream schools would be considered as the first choice for all young people including those deemed to have additional support needs The Scottish Executive in 'Moving Forward! Additional Support for Learning' (SEED 2003) took this vision of inclusion on board and emphasised that inclusive schools 'welcome pupil diversity and develop an ethos and values which promote the educational, social and cultural development of all pupils' (p. 22). Notwithstanding the fact that commitment to inclusion in mainstream schools is a priority in Scottish education, for some young people the mainstream environment may not be conducive to meeting their needs. There will therefore continue to be a need for more diverse forms of provision, and for the foreseeable future specialist provision outwith mainstream schools will be a vital requirement. It is important to understand that whereas inclusion is firmly linked to mainstreaming and the ultimate aim is to have the majority of young people in mainstream contexts, these are not as yet one and the same thing. Fundamentally inclusion is about educating young people in the environment which best meets their needs and that might require some form of specialist provision particularly in the case of those whose additional support needs are more severe or complex.

Mainstreaming

Section 15 of the 2000 Act put a responsibility on Scottish education authorities to provide education in mainstream schools for all young people. However it is also recognised in this Act that the mainstream may not be the most appropriate learning environment for all and so three conditions have been built in. A young person might not be included in mainstream when:

- the mainstream is not suited to his/her level of ability
- the young person would disrupt the learning of others
- high levels of expenditure would be involved.

Although it is recommended that these conditions should apply only in exceptional circumstances it is easy to see how they might, without very careful monitoring, be open to misuse. Nonetheless it is now accepted throughout Scottish education that the mainstream school will now be the first choice for all young people with additional support needs. This presumption of mainstreaming is now firmly enshrined in law and highlights the purpose of inclusive education as maximising the participation of all young people in mainstream schools, and the removal of attitudinal and structural barriers.

Another principle which has strongly influenced the development of more inclusive mainstream school cultures can be traced back to the civil rights movement of the 1960s. It is now clear that the promotion of human rights is central to effective inclusion. All individuals have rights, and the rights of young people have now been recognised as very important. Article 2 of the United Nations Convention on the Rights of the Child (1989) emphasises that rights apply to all children without exception. This view was elaborated within the Children (Scotland) Act (1995) and has impacted upon all subsequent legislation pertaining to inclusion. Many of the professionals who write about and engage in research in relation to inclusion focus upon this issue of rights (Clough 1998; Allan 1999; Hamill and Boyd 2002) and present it as an important factor in making mainstream inclusion a reality.

Hall (1997) is a forceful advocate in relation to what he sees as the right of all young people, regardless of the nature and range of their additional needs, to attend their local mainstream school. He suggests that any form of segregation is culturally deviant and that it is morally wrong to block access to the mainstream school for any young person. On the other hand Corbett (1998) sounds a cautionary note when she says that we must take care not to get sidetracked into an ideological battlefield where meeting individual needs can all too often be lost in the relentless drive towards mainstream inclusion at all cost. It is important to keep in mind that the vision of mainstream inclusion and the reality are still not yet one and the same thing. Change takes place slowly and although the concept of total mainstream inclusion is a goal we continue to strive for it is still to a large extent an ideological vision which will continue to provide the framework for evolving legislation, policy and practice.

The 'Count Us In' Report (SEED 2003) makes it very clear that implementing the broader view of inclusion will require professionals who are innovative and who are capable of meeting a range of challenges. These include catering for a wide range of diverse needs, supporting alienated and/or disaffected pupils and developing forms of specialist provision as part of an inclusive school system. The features of inclusive practice are listed on page 4 of this report as follows:

- creating an ethos of achievement for all pupils within a climate of high expectation
- valuing a broad range of talents, abilities and achievements
- promoting success and self-esteem by taking action to remove barriers to learning
- countering conscious and unconscious discrimination that may prevent individuals, from any particular groups, from thriving within the school
- actively promoting understanding and a positive appreciation of diversity of individuals and groups within society.

Putting these principles into practice is not easy; schools striving to create inclusive cultures must be prepared to subject all of their systems and structures to scrutiny.

Specialist provision

Specialist provision outwith mainstream has been part of the Scottish education system for many years and it is very important to consider the relationship between special schools and the drive towards inclusion. The report 'Moving Forward! Additional Support for Learning' (SEED 2003) acknowledges the continuing need for diversity of provision. In 2002 according to the Scottish Executive Summary results of the 2001 school census, specialist provision in Scotland comprised 197 publicly funded special schools and units, containing 8,183 young people. In the independent sector there were 33 special schools with 1,038 pupils, and around 400 young people attended grant-aided special schools. The overall number of young people assessed as having special educational needs was 44,000. Thus it is clear that in reality the majority of young people with additional support needs are already in mainstream schools and the legal presumption that mainstream will be the first choice for a young person will continue to have an impact on the role and function of special provision outwith mainstream.

It is interesting to note that since 2000 there has been increasing pressure put upon those who advocate inclusion to provide evidence that it is effective. This contrasts with the fact that, despite special schools having existed for many years, little research has been done in relation to their efficacy. Instead it has simply been assumed that special schools are the best learning environments for some young people. This claim is usually based on two arguments which have never really been subjected to rigorous academic scrutiny:

- special school teachers usually have some form of additional training
- the staff–pupil ratio is lower.

It is now recognised that there is a need to set up comparative studies looking at the impact of different forms of provision on young people. Hegarty (1991) points out that disabling conditions make matching the needs of these learners difficult and make the creation of control groupings virtually impossible.

Having said this, however, there is now a small but significant body of research evidence emerging which suggests that the benefits of inclusion may outweigh placement in special schools. Buckley *et al.* (2000) compared provision in Hampshire for young people with Downs Syndrome. Although the sample was fairly small they did find that those young people who attended mainstream school were significantly more advanced in relation to expressive language, reading, writing, arithmetic and general knowledge. While acknowledging weaknesses in making comparisons, several other research studies tend to support Buckley's conclusions. Dew, Hughes and Blanford (1998) focused on young people deemed to have severe and complex needs and considered in particular their social development and independent learning skills. In the mainstream context these young people tended to be more autonomous and worked co-operatively for longer periods. The researchers linked this success to teacher expectation and found that many special school teachers tended to have lower expectations. A further longitudinal study carried out in America tracking the post-school experiences of 8,000 young people found that young people with physical disabilities educated in mainstream schools were more likely to gain employment than those educated in special schools. There is therefore a growing body of research providing evidence which raises serious questions about the future of special schools; this will be considered in more depth in Chapter 8.

It would appear that the move towards inclusion is based on sound principles such as entitlement, equality and rights. However, the challenge of implementing these in practice cannot be underestimated and we must continue to find research evidence which shows that inclusion is working. Lipsky and Gartner (1996) examined around 20 UK studies which focused on the success of social and academic inclusion in mainstream settings. Further evidence to support this comes from Salend and Duhaney (1999) who found that young people with disabilities educated in mainstream settings improved in relation to standardised tests, motivation and grades. The staff involved also reported an improvement in attitudes towards school and learning, and more positive interaction with peers. Benefits for these non-disabled peers were highlighted by Manset and Semmel (1997) who concluded that when schools adapt to cater more effectively for disabled students non-disabled young people are positively affected by these changes.

It would be premature to state conclusively that inclusion is the answer for all young people, and the debate will continue for some time yet as research findings emerge. What is clear at present is that professionals have to present a strong case for educating a young person in a special school outwith the mainstream and, as emerging legislation continues to support inclusion, pressure will certainly be placed on those who make decisions of this nature to justify them.

Developing inclusive school cultures

In 1996 the Centre for Studies in Inclusive Education (CSIE) compiled a descriptive profile which outlined the features of an inclusive school. It emphasised that such a school was community based, barrier free and collaboration and equality were key themes permeating all levels of school life. An inclusive school should not be selective, exclusive or rejecting, and above all it should be democratic, providing opportunity for all. School managers and education authorities must be prepared to actively embrace the process of inclusion as having the power to transform systems for the benefit of all, and to fund the means to achieve this. Much of the literature on inclusion concentrates on the potential of inclusion policies to restructure schools and make them more responsive to the diversity of learning needs. Hamill and Boyd (2000, 2001, 2002) found that in reality many schools were still viewing inclusion as fitting the young person into existing systems rather than reforming systems to meet their needs. These findings support the work of Dyson (1997) who concluded that inclusion had to a large extent simply resulted in the setting up of colonies of young people within mainstream schools as opposed to transforming mainstream education: 'Whilst attempting to include children with special needs in regular classes, special education to date has merely reproduced itself in a mainstream setting' (p. 154) An inclusive school culture will never become a reality in schools where the management team have not themselves fully internalised its potential for changing systems for the better and are unable to share this vision with their staff. Inclusion means change and the process of change can sometimes be uncomfortable and threatening.

In inclusive schools all young people are able to access an appropriate curriculum, and it is through the curriculum that messages are sent and received about the value and status of individuals (Swann 1988). This is often done through the hidden curriculum where young people learn about things like sex role differentiation, bureaucracy, authority and equality. Since the early 1980s teachers in Scottish schools have, through research, educational reports and legislation, consistently been told that the curriculum itself can be the source of learning and behavioural difficulties as well as have the potential to alleviate difficulties. It has been painful for some teachers to realise that some young people may not learn effectively due to a mismatch between the delivery of the curriculum and the young person's learning needs. Teachers who are effective at including and supporting all young people understand that the inclusive curriculum is a powerful tool in promoting opportunity for all, including those with additional support needs.

However, as Solity (1993) points out, planning and delivering a curriculum that can be accessed by all is a complex and skilful process. In practice, for the reflective teacher, emphasis is on the provision of meaningful and relevant learning experiences. It is clear that learners have a variety of needs, which need to be addressed in different ways, and differentiation is the curricular strategy which caters for this variation. It applies to all effective teaching and is the key to an inclusive curriculum. In an inclusive culture, staff have internalised the principles that underpin differentiation and see it as a strategy for raising attainment. Ultimately differentiation is about effective teaching and learning. It is about doing what we can at class level before resorting to exclusion. Catering for diversity through differentiation can be challenging but it is at the core of inclusive practice and is one strategy professionals can use to help them meet the challenge of inclusion.

Since the mid 1980s curricular reform has been high on the educational agenda in Scotland. The 5–14 programme, for example, now provides a curricular framework which emphasises the principles of coherence, breadth, balance and continuity. The professionals who shaped this programme were keen to ensure that the needs of young people requiring additional support were seen to be central. The 5–14 programme applies to all young people regardless of the context in which they learn and highlights the fact that all young people are entitled to a curriculum which is broad, balanced and effectively differentiated. This presents teachers with the need to challenge and change traditional practices and thus they have to reconcile two juxtaposed curricular requirements, i.e.

- the aims of education should apply to all young people, irrespective of their level of ability or the school they attend
- the differences in each individual's needs, abilities and aspirations must be taken into account.

Reconciling these two requirements is not easy and it can be argued that many teachers have not as yet internalised this view. They continue to advocate a separate special curriculum for those who have additional support needs, a different curriculum from that of their peers.

The ethos and culture within schools and classrooms is crucial to effective inclusion, and much of the literature on school effectiveness has highlighted these issues. In 1997 the report 'How Good is Our School' focused on quality assurance within the education system and considered how schools could develop a culture of quality by 'establishing an ethos that only the best will do and that by working together we can make significant improvements' (SOEID 1997, p. 3). The school effectiveness movement has also played its part in raising awareness of factors that characterise an inclusive school culture. These include senior managers incorporating into their development planning the need to promote a vision of inclusion permeating all levels, particularly policies on teaching and learning, organisational change and curriculum delivery. Inclusion will depend to a large extent on whether or not strong effective leadership is in place. Sebba and Ainscow (1996) outline what they see as a few vital prerequisites: the encouragement of mixed-ability groupings where possible, cooperative and active learning, interprofessional collaboration and a differentiated curriculum. Where these factors are central to the development of a school, they not only result in more effective learning environments for all but characterise inclusive school cultures. Where they tend to be peripheral, the school is likely to be less responsive to the principle of inclusion. Young people experience the reality of inclusion first and foremost in the classroom where the teacher creates an environment in which everyone is valued. Effective inclusion is inextricably linked to effective teaching and it is therefore important that we consider some of the qualities that an inclusive teacher possesses.

The Inclusive Teacher

The key to inclusion is in the hands of the classroom teacher and it is not surprising to find that the inclusive teacher draws on the same skills and attitudes that made her an effective teacher in the first place. If we wish to know what these are then asking young people for their views seems a logical place to start. This was the approach taken by Hamill and Boyd in all three of their studies of inclusion within Scottish schools. The Standards in Scotland's Schools etc. Act (2000) reinforced the fact that young people in Scotland now have participation rights which give them a say in decisions taken on matters which affect them. These rights include actively seeking their views in relation to school development and education authority plans. Hamill and Boyd interviewed around 500 young people; and approximately 25% of these young people were deemed to be disaffected, alienated and marginalised and were consistently excluded from school because of their challenging behaviour. These young people had additional support needs linked to social, emotional and behavioural difficulties. The remaining 75% of young people interviewed had never been excluded and many of them were very able young people who served on the Pupil Council in their schools. The researchers found that these young people had a lot to say about their teachers and the role they played in creating inclusive classroom cultures. There was ample evidence to suggest that the vast majority understood how complex and stressful the teacher's job could be and spoke highly of the many teachers who in their opinion do a first class job. One boy in S2 summed this up as follows 'The teacher's job can be really hard. They have to try and help everyone and everyone wants this or that at the same time. It's hard for the teacher to cope.'

These young people did not of course refer to the 'inclusive teacher' but they did consistently refer to those they perceived as effective i.e. 'good teachers'. When the researchers teased out what this meant they concluded that the young people were expressing in their own language the view that the most effective teachers made the effort to include and value everyone. Three words which cropped up time and time again in relation to the good teacher were 'equality', 'fairness' and 'rights'. This reinforces a view that often emerges from the literature on inclusive schools: that one major indicator of inclusive schools is the extent to which everyone within them is valued and treated equally (Thomas, Walker and Webb 1998). These young people also expressed views that revealed that the theory of equality did not, as far as some teachers were concerned, always translate into practice. An S4 girl made this point very clearly when she said 'a lot of teachers do try to treat everyone equally but it is not true that all pupils in this school are equally valued. Some teachers convey a sense that they don't like pupils and treat you as if you are not worth bothering about.'

Hamill and Boyd (2002) were able to draw up a checklist of the factors that young people most associated with the inclusive teacher; these are outlined in Table 2.1.

Table 2.1 The inclusive teacher

• Listens to you and encourages you
• Has faith in you and makes time for you
• Likes teaching children and their subject
• Explains things and helps you when you are stuck
• Allows you to have your say and cares about your opinion
• Makes you feel clever not stupid
• Treats everyone fairly and equally
• Is strict and makes you work but also has a sense of humour
• Gives you interesting work and tries to make learning fun

Most of these factors appear at first glance to be common sense. However these young people took great pains to emphasise that in their opinion not all teachers met these criteria. One very articulate young man spoke for many of his peers when he said 'good teachers understand how you feel; they respect you and don't automatically assume they are always right. Bad teachers don't listen, treat you like dirt, boss you around all the time and think they are always right.'

In addition to the factors outlined in Table 2.1, Hamill and Boyd have also drawn up a list of indicators that a teacher can use as part of a self-evaluation exercise in relation to inclusive practice. These are presented in Table 2.2.

Table 2.2 Inclusion – teacher self-evaluation

- I avoid negatively labelling and stereotyping young people
- I appreciate that the curriculum can be a source of learning/behavioural difficulties
- I am prepared to reflect upon my own behaviour as well as that of the young person
- I make a conscious effort to apply the principle of equality to all young people
- I am aware of the hidden curriculum and its impact on young people
- I work hard to ensure the ethos in my classroom is positive and everyone is valued
- I take every opportunity to work collaboratively with others
- I agree that as far as possible mainstream schools should include all young people
- I take every opportunity to enhance the self-esteem of the young people I teach
- I welcome diversity in young people and cater for it through differentiation
- I respect all professionals and value the contribution they make
- I welcome parents and treat them equally
- All young people in my class are given a voice and I listen to them
- I always adopt a child-centred as opposed to a subject-centred approach
- I relate well to my colleagues and am happy to listen to and take advice from them
- I work hard to create a learning environment which is stimulating/motivating
- I treat all young people the way I would want members of my family treated
- I actively try to support colleagues who may need help.
- I am enthusiastic and committed to the subject(s) I teach
- I only pass problems to senior management after I have tried to resolve them myself

If inclusion is to become a reality in schools, teachers need to internalise an inclusive philosophy which translates into practice. Actions speak louder than words and it is not possible to fool the young people we teach. We must always remember the power of the hidden curriculum. It is not possible to stand in front of a class of young people, day in day out, without conveying to them the extent to which you do or do not respect and value them as human beings. This is the true hallmark of inclusion.

SUMMARY

Inclusion is now high on the educational agenda in Scotland. It remains, however, the topic of debate and is acknowledged by most professionals as a complex, multi-faceted concept. All too often inclusion is simply equated with including young people with additional support needs in mainstream schools. This is, of course, a very important dimension of inclusion but in reality it is a much more diverse concept.

Mainstreaming and inclusion are very closely related. The overall aim is to include all young people in mainstream as far as possible. However, for some young people this may not be feasible and therefore specialist provision outwith mainstream will continue to be the most appropriate environment for them.

An inclusive school embraces a wide range of learners and provides opportunities for all. Such schools require inclusive teachers, and successful inclusion will depend largely on the willingness and ability of these teachers to translate inclusive principles into practice. For many teachers, effective resourcing is at the heart of the inclusion debate, and continuing professional development which enables the teachers' voice to be heard is also recognised as an important factor. Most teachers accept the theory underpinning inclusion but have questions about how it will be implemented in reality.

POINTS FOR REFLECTION

1 What is inclusion? Do all of the significant individuals (i.e. young people, teachers, parents, and other professionals) share an understanding of this term or is it still open to confusion and misinterpretation?

2 The presumption of mainstream education as far as is possible for young people with additional support needs is now enshirined in Scottish law. Are inclusion and mainstreaming one and the same thing?

3 What characteristics would be in evidence in a school which had successfully developed an inclusive culture and ethos? What personal and professional qualities should an inclusive teacher possess?

3 Additional support needs: an overview

 Respect for the fragility and importance of an individual life is still the first mark of an educated man.

Norman Cousins

Introduction

The Scottish Executive Education Department (SEED 2003a) identified five national priorities for education and, in Scotland, we are now moving towards an implementation of the changes essential to ensuring that these priorities are addressed. It would be helpful to consider these priorities as the framework of education being developed and streamlined to support the education of all children and young people in Scotland. These priorities, which are the keystones of educational improvement in Scotland, are: Achievement and Attainment; Framework for Learning; Inclusion and Equality; Values and Citizenship; and Learning for Life.

Children and young people with "additional support needs", a term which will be considered in more detail in this chapter, are represented within that framework. The national priorities have been set for *all* children and young people, including those with additional support needs, so each keystone applies to them too. 'Achievement and Attainment' is about success for all. The 'Framework for Learning' has an emphasis on support for all. 'Inclusion and equality' considers how schools can become more inclusive contexts which provide improved access to the curriculum for all. 'Values and Citizenship' has the rights of all children at its core and 'Learning for Life' considers the needs of all young people as they move on beyond school education.

An exciting new blueprint has been drawn up to ensure the strength of this framework for education in Scotland. Additional support needs are clearly set within and across each of the keystones that make up this framework. The legislation which is detailed in the next section of this chapter should be viewed in the context of the framework already described.

Legislation

The response to a national consultation exercise by the Scottish Executive (2002) laid the foundation from which the new Education (Additional Support for Learning) (Scotland) Act (2004) emerged. This consultation exercise focused on identifying the changes that would be necessary to improve and update the assessment and recording process for children and young people with special educational needs.

As a result the Scottish Executive Education Department (SEED 2003a), following wide consultation on proposals for change, proposed that new legislation with changed terminology should be introduced. This legislation (Scottish Parliament 2004) would be based on the concept of additional support needs, with the aim of representing a more flexible, positive and inclusive approach to providing support for learning. The philosophy which underpinned it was based on the premise that all children need support to learn but some have additional support needs. These children will be those who face barriers to learning which call for more specific provision to be made to enable them to overcome the barriers and achieve progress in their learning.

Within the Act, a child or young person has additional support needs when he/she 'is, or is likely to be, unable without the provision of additional support, to benefit from school education provided, or to be provided for the child or young person' (Scottish Parliament 2004, section 1). The legislation aims to cover the additional support needs of all children and young people in school education, from pre-school to secondary, and also children who are under school age and not in pre-school education. In the case of the latter, there may still be some educational provision such as home-visiting teachers.

The new legislative framework has been designed to update and strengthen the system for providing additional support for learning so that all children who experience barriers to learning are identified and supported in the learning process. It is intended that parents' involvement in decisions about their children's education will also be strengthened. The proposed changes centre on the following key features:

- replacement of the current assessment and recording system (Record of Needs) with a strengthened but streamlined, intervention process;
- a new flexible Co-ordinated Support Plan (CSP) for children who face long-term complex or multiple barriers to learning and who require frequent access to a diversity of services from outwith education;
- a new requirement for local authorities to have mediation services in place for early resolution of disputes;
- extended rights of appeal for parents of children with a CSP to allow them to challenge the level of provision proposed; and
- the establishment of an independent tribunal to hear appeals.

(SEED 2003a, p. 11)

In the future all children and young people who have additional support needs must have their needs identified and have appropriate support for their learning. However, not all of these children and young people will have an entitlement to a Co-ordinated Support Plan (CSP):

> The CSP is for those children and young persons with enduring additional support needs arising from complex or multiple factors for whose school education the education authority are responsible, who require support from a range of providers... ...Services additional to education could, for example, be therapy services provided by NHS or respite care from social work services.
> (Scottish Parliament 2003, section 26, p. 7).

To ensure that education authorities comply with the new legislation, a code of practice and directions will be issued to education authorities to enable them to understand the duty placed on them by the new legislation and to provide them with guidance in the execution of their duty. Compliance with the legislation, and the code of practice and directions, is essential (Scottish Parliament 2004, section 27). The code of practice includes guidance on:

- the particular circumstances, or factors, which may give rise to additional support needs
- the identification of complex and multiple factors

- the nature of the additional support to be provided within a CSP
- the nature of the additional support which may be required
- the arrangements to be made for children and young people with additional support needs
- the seeking of information, advice and views from relevant agencies, parties and the children and young people themselves
- the arrangements to be made for mediation services
- how to carry out their duties with regard to placing requests
- when circumstances determine that such duties do not apply.

(adapted from Scottish Parliament 2004, Section 27 (2))

The challenge of diversity

In a study by Clark, Cooper and Ross-Watt (2004), which focused on inclusion in pre-school and primary school settings within one Scottish education authority, a picture emerged of some schools and nurseries which were at the beginning of their journey towards inclusion and others which had truly embraced the philosophy and the ideal of this concept. In the case of the former, negative views of inclusion were expressed by staff and, in the latter case, staff had initiated planned, active and often dynamic change to ensure that an inclusive, supportive environment for pupils and staff existed. Teachers' attitudes and belief systems had a strong influence in both scenarios.

At both ends of the spectrum described above, and in schools which were at varying points along the way, management and staff felt challenged by inclusion because of the widening range of significant needs which were reflected by their pupils. Even in those establishments where staff were supportive of inclusion, there was a perception that there was insufficient training, staffing and resources to make available adequate support to ensure that all pupils had the best learning experiences. The main concern among staff was a strong feeling that they had not been trained at initial teacher education level to cope with such a wide range of pupil needs. An earlier study by Clark (2001) undertaken in the era of integration had also uncovered similar views and perceptions.

Inclusion does present a challenge. As the population of learners in inclusive contexts grows to include those with significant additional support needs, staff in schools are likely to feel threatened by the resulting changes both to the teaching context and to their styles of teaching, unless they themselves are supported in their endeavours to ensure that every pupil attains his/her potential. Continuing professional development for teachers, particularly the Chartered Teacher Programme, offers an opportunity for teachers to feel that they have ownership of their own personal and professional needs and aspirations. Such professional development is likely to promote change in schools, as discussed by McNiff (1993).

Barriers to learning

As stated earlier, children and young people who have additional support needs face barriers to their learning, which can arise from the interactions between pupils and learning contexts. Understanding such barriers will enable schools and their staff to develop and extend their inclusive practice (Cowne 2003). Ethos, attitudes and teacher value systems have a part to play in ensuring that all pupils feel welcome and valued in school. If these aspects are less than positive then schools are likely to be less than inclusive and pupils will experience barriers to learning.

Some barriers to learning may arise from social and environmental factors, such as poverty, which place pupils at an educational disadvantage. In these circumstances pupils' knowledge and understanding of the world may require enrichment and enhancement. If a compensatory model of education, aimed at such enrichment and enhancement, is not set in operation by the school, such additional support needs will continue to create barriers to learning when pupils try to interact with their peers and the curriculum, because they lack the grounding and necessary skills to succeed in their learning.

Differing abilities must be catered for within classrooms. Pace of learning, volume of work and time allotted to tasks are some of the factors that must be considered when differentiating work for pupils. If support needs are not taken into account then barriers to pupils' learning will be created within the curriculum. Where pupils do not have the required skills to achieve success in tasks that are set by the teacher, the tasks themselves become barriers to learning. Interrupted education will result in gaps in learning: pupils who have been absent for periods of time will find it difficult to bridge the inevitable gaps in their learning without support. If there is no mechanism within the school system which enables them to be supported in such cases then this will result in them experiencing barriers to learning.

The teacher's job is to support all pupils in their learning. In order to do this successfully teachers must know about the strengths and learning needs of all of their pupils. Planning must be targeted to take these strengths and needs into account. In this way assessment and planning go hand in hand. Assessment must be an integral part of the teaching. Teachers should be making observations and adjustments to plans on a continuous basis. Such a model is child-centred with the teacher as problem-solver, trying to find solutions or strategies to reduce barriers to school learning in order that children find success and can cope in the school context. (Cowne 2003).

Where the additional support needs are more enduring, multiple or complex, teachers will need support from specialist teachers and other agencies in order to try to reduce barriers to pupils' learning. A collaborative approach will be essential in such circumstances as these pupils are most likely to be those who will have a Co-ordinated Support Plan (CSP). Time to collaborate can be problematic but it is vital that finding this time should be a school priority in such cases in the same way as it has been for the review process in respect of the Record of Needs (RON). This model of extended support requires schools to have a clearly articulated whole-school policy on support for learning which has been clearly communicated to, and understood by, all staff so that they have ownership of the process involved in inter-agency collaboration. The stages in such a process must take account of the roles and responsibilities of all parties involved in the process.

Additional support needs: casting the net more widely

As reported by the Scottish Executive (SEED 2003b), a wide-ranging set of circumstances has been identified which could impact on a pupil's learning and give rise to additional support needs, although not all of these will necessarily be in themselves barriers to pupils' learning. The circumstances should, however, be known to schools so that allowances can be made and/or support can be put in place. The list presented in Table 3.1 was compiled by the Scottish Executive (SEED 2003b). It is not an exhaustive one but certainly contains some circumstances which were not considered within the former framework of special educational needs.

Table 3.1 Circumstances which may give rise to additional support needs

- Children with Attention Deficit (Hyperactivity) Disorder
- Children with Autistic Spectrum Disorder
- Children who have suffered a bereavement in family
- Children who are bullying or being bullied
- Children adopted or in the process of being adopted
- Children in need of protection
- Child, parent or family member has been victim or witness of serious crime
- Children who are carers for relatives or who are affected by disability
- Children who live in violent environments
- Children whose health and development is suffering
- Children whose parents suffer from a mental illness
- Children whose educational development is suffering (including those excluded)
- Children whose parents misuse substances/alcohol
- Children/young people in poor housing
- Children/young people no longer looked after
- Children/young people who are in conflict with the law because of offending behaviour
- Children/young people affected by HIV/AIDS
- Children with disabilities
- Children with disfigurement
- Children with divorcing/separating parents
- Children with dyslexia
- Children with dyspraxia
- Children with English as an additional language
- Gifted or able children whose learning potential is being hindered
- Children who have suffered interrupted learning e.g. through long stay in hospital, gypsy or traveller families
- Children who have suffered language or communication disorders
- Children whose parent or family member is in prison
- Children with sensory impairments
- Children with temporary medical conditions
- Children with terminal illness
- Children who are young carers/young parents

(adapted from SEED 2003b, p. 37)

Some pupils may need additional support for a relatively short period of time. Others may need support for much longer, in some cases throughout a pupil's entire period of school education. All pupils identified as having additional support needs should have an Individualised Educational Programme (IEP). Since 2003 all pupils, including those with additional support needs, should have a Personal Learning Plan (PLP) (Scottish Executive 2002). The PLP will provide an ongoing assessment tool, record and action plan based on pupils' and families' active involvement in identifying pupil learning outcomes. For those pupils who have additional support needs, the essential, detailed, child-centred planning which forms the essence of an IEP will continue and the IEP will become part of the PLP (SEED 2003a, p.15). Further guidance on the PLP process is currently being developed by SEED in collaboration with Learning and Teaching Scotland.

The Co-ordinated Support Plan (CSP) is a working document aimed at ensuring that a multi-agency approach to provision of support is set up and maintained for those who have the most enduring complex and/or multiple needs. As a working document, it is intended to inform provision of support and can be adapted and changed as a pupil's needs alter. All agencies involved with the child or young person will have access to the CSP. Section 7 of the Education (Additional Support for Learning) (Scotland) Act (2004) gives some indication of the proposed content and format of the CSP:

- The reason for the individual's additional support needs and a description of his/her difficulties must be detailed. In addition the young person's skills and capabilities will be noted.
- The learning outcomes to be achieved should be included.
- Details of the additional support needed to achieve the planned learning outcomes and a note of who will provide this support.
- The school the individual is to attend must be noted.
- Information about the nominated person who will co-ordinate the plan must be recorded.
- Contact information for a named officer from whom information and advice may be sought must be included.
- The plan is likely to contain biographical details of the young person and may also include contact details for the young person, and his parent or carer.

- It is likely that everyone involved in drawing up the plan will be expected to sign it to acknowledge their input, and a timescale to review the plan will be included.
- There may be an annex to the CSP which will be used to record progress towards achieving the learning outcomes.

Education authorities will have a duty to co-ordinate the support provided as set out in the CSP, and the manager of the day-to-day implementation of the CSP will be named in the CSP. Such a person could be a health worker or a social worker who may be deemed to be more appropriate if they have wider involvement with the family (SEED 2003b, p. 29). Inter-agency working can itself be problematic because each agency has its own aims, priorities, use of language/terminology and culture. However, a good model of inter-agency working which has been instrumental in streamlining the provision for many young children in Scotland has been the Pre-School Community Assessment Team (Pre-SCAT) process. Within this model, education, health and social work professionals have successfully worked collaboratively to ensure that the needs of pre-school children and their families have been taken into account when making decisions about placement and levels of support. If this model can be adapted in trying to meet the needs of children with, or likely to have, a CSP at any stage in their school education then the process of such inter-agency collaboration should be less problematic. The criteria which promote the success of such ventures are discussed by Roaf (2001).

Complex and multiple factors

As we have seen, the Co-ordinated Support Plan will be drawn up for those young people who experience long-term complex or multiple factors which can pose barriers to learning. It is therefore very important that everyone involved in the CSP process shares an understanding of what constitutes complex or multiple factors that might impede learning

Complex factors

A complex factor which is likely to merit a CSP is one that affects most aspects of learning. This may be a long-term educational, medical or other factor, such as:

- a significant sensory impairment (hearing or vision)
- severe intellectual learning difficulties
- Autistic Spectrum Disorder
- physical disability which impacts on learning (this could be as a result of cerebral palsy when it affects communication, for example)
- Attention Deficit Hyperactivity Disorder (ADHD).

Each of the above, depending on the severity of the impact on the education process, will require pupils to have additional support for their learning, including support from other agencies. One or more complex factors may be present in any one pupil profile.

Multiple factors

Multiple factors are a combination of two or more factors which can be educational, medical, social, behavioural, or other factors. Each by itself may not be a complex factor but in combination may have the same effect on learning as a complex factor. If a pupil is a young carer, for example, whose health and development is suffering and whose educational development is suffering because of interrupted learning, then such a pupil would be deemed to have multiple factors which give rise to additional support needs. The support required for this pupil is likely to come from health, social work and education co-ordinated through a CSP.

Information about complex and multiple factors is considered by the SEED (2003b) and within Section 2 of the Education (Additional Support for Learning) (Scotland) Act (2004).

Implications for the future

By casting the net more widely, it is hoped that the additional support needs of a very wide range of pupils will be considered and acknowledged by schools. This does not mean that there will necessarily be an increase in the number of pupils who require a CSP as opposed to a Record of Needs (RON), since inclusion is not a new phenomenon. However, there will be a need for schools to have access to information which in many cases can be sensitive and highly confidential. Schools will have to consider how they should manage and store such information.

Plans for individual pupils are actioned by class teachers in collaboration with a range of professionals, parents and support staff, who should know about the important details of the additional support needs of the pupils at the centre of the plan. Issues of confidentiality and disclosure are very sensitive ones. School management, with guidance from education authorities, must decide who should know what, and how much detail is required.

Staff development is key to providing staff with the knowledge and understanding which will enable them to respond appropriately to more diverse pupil needs. If more individuals require individualised planning, albeit within a shared learning context, there is a big time factor implication for the classroom teacher and for all staff who plan collaboration with him/her.

A number of the circumstances which may give rise to pupils having additional support needs (see Table 3.1) will already be known to social work and or health professionals, but not in every case. Teachers and support staff in schools will have to understand the educational implications of such circumstances in order to have empathy with the pupils concerned, and make allowances for them. Some general principles will apply in certain cases but individuals cope differently with the same set of circumstances so general principles should be applied advisedly.

When pupils are coping with a problem that causes anxiety or stress, such as bereavement, terminal illness in the family, or divorcing parents, teachers should make allowances to reduce the pupils' stress and/or anxiety. Pressure of work should be reduced either by providing more time for tasks or fewer examples to be done, encouraging the pupil to talk about their feelings and how they are coping. Teachers should take advice from other professionals where necessary in such circumstances, under the guidance of management in the school.

Teachers need to know about the educational implications of certain complex factors which may or may not merit the pupil having a CSP. The important point to remember is that the complex factor in itself should not become the barrier to the pupil's progress. If the effects on learning are known, then teachers can plan appropriately to meet the needs of the individual. Dyslexia, dyspraxia, ADHD, Autistic Spectrum Disorder, and a range of disabilities and language and communication disorders have been written about extensively.

Teachers should be encouraged to develop their personal and professional knowledge and understanding of such specific difficulties when necessary and to seek the support and advice of specialist support-for-learning staff when planning to meet the additional support needs of pupils with such difficulties.

Within the Chartered Teacher Programme, opportunities to focus on some of these specific difficulties will be afforded via the option modules.

SUMMARY

The five national priorities for education in Scotland are focused on an education for all children including those with additional support needs. The concept of additional support needs is wider than the previous concept of special educational needs and the new legislation is designed to represent diversity of children's needs and guarantee them support within the education system. Teachers must be made aware of the range of barriers to children's learning. In responding to children's needs, teachers are expected to work collaboratively with a range of professionals who represent not only education but also health and social work. New skills and greater understanding will be required by all involved in this process. Training and awareness of the implications of the new legislation will be key to ensuring that all involved in responding to children's additional support needs can respond appropriately to the challenges presented by inclusion within the new legislative framework.

POINTS FOR REFLECTION

1 What are the five national priorities for education in Scotland? Do staff in schools, and other relevant professionals, know that pupils with additional support needs are represented within and across these priorities?

2 How aware are staff in schools, and other relevant professionals, of the new legislation which underpins the concept of additional support needs? What will be the impact of this legislation on practice in schools?

3 To what extent do schools acknowledge that barriers to learning can be generated within the curriculum and by teachers in classrooms? Are we prepared in our schools to effectively support the needs of a wider range of pupils in collaboration with other relevant professionals?

4 Principles underpinning good practice in supporting young people with additional support needs

> **"** The theories and goals of education don't matter a whit if you don't consider your students as human beings. **"**
> **Lou Ann Walker**

There are undoubtedly common principles which underpin good practice in relation to additional support needs, regardless of the context in which the young person is educated. If the support provided is to be effective it must be set within a framework where all professionals have internalised a set of principles that inform practice. In 2003 the Scottish Executive outlined in the report 'Moving Forward! Additional Support for Learning' what they described as their vision for the future and presented some key principles which supported this vision. These are outlined in Table 4.1.

Table 4.1 Key principles

- Education must be *child-centred*, yet take a holistic approach to the needs of the child and his/her family.

- Allocation of resources by schools, local authorities and their partners should demonstrate a commitment to inclusiveness and the delivery of *integrated services* and take account of the *diversity of* local pupil populations.

- National and local policies for improving *standards* should include *all* children.

- The *rights* and *views* of young people and their parents should be respected and listened to.

- Schools should demonstrate a commitment to *inclusiveness*.

All of these key principles are multi-faceted and to fully understand the extent to which they inform practice within schools it is important to consider each in a bit more depth. Therefore the aim of this chapter is to shed some light on each principle and to provide guidance to schools that are keen to ensure they are translating these principles into practice.

A child-centred approach

Few teachers would dispute the fact that their job is first and foremost child-centred as opposed to subject-centred. This implies therefore that both learning and teaching are organic human processes based firmly within a teacher–learner relationship where the challenge is matching teaching style to learning needs.

Creating the environment where all learners can thrive is not easy because learners do not fall neatly into homogenous groups. Firstly they vary considerably intellectually, socially, physically and aesthetically. They also differ in their emotional development, levels of motivation, interests, health, personality and upbringing. In short, young people are human, they do not all fit the same mould, and the task for any teacher is to find ways to cater for this diversity. Differentiation is the means of achieving this aim. It is not a new concept and has been around for a fairly long time. Although all teachers have heard about it, differentiation has, to some extent, simply become a buzz word which remains at the level of rhetoric, and in many schools it has never become a reality. O'Brien and Guiney (2001) talk about the link between learning needs and differentiation and present a needs model which can be applied to learners in any classroom. This model helps us to understand that the concept of learning need is complex and presents challenges for the teacher. O'Brien and Guiney (2001, p. 15) identify three levels of need:

- common needs – everyone is the same
- distinct needs – some people are similar
- individual needs – everyone is different.

Differentiation first emerged in the late 1970s as a concept which was almost synonymous with those young people now described as having additional support needs. Adapting the curriculum to meet their individual needs tended to be an afterthought as opposed to a central concern at the planning stage, and at that time many professionals held the view that a common curriculum already existed which met the needs of the majority. The task in hand was to simply find ways to adapt the existing curriculum to cater for these special children with additional support needs. It is within this context that the process of curricular differentiation evolved and came to be seen as focusing on the few who were seen to be different as opposed to being seen as a process crucial to the effective learning of all young people. Thus differentiation became firmly established within the minds of many professionals as a process relating to a clearly defined group of learners identified as having fundamentally different needs from their peers.

It is not difficult to understand why the concept of differentiation has come to be so closely linked to those whose learning difficulties mean they have additional support needs. The 1978 HMI report which focused on the education of pupils with learning difficulties alerted schools to the fact that around 20% of learners were unable to access the curriculum on offer. This seminal report was the first to raise the possibility of the curriculum itself as a source of learning difficulty and promoted differentiation as the key to an accessible curriculum. Unfortunately the commitment to, and enthusiasm for, differentiation was not as contagious as had been hoped for and differentiation, like many young people with additional support needs, remained on the periphery as opposed to becoming central to the education of all learners.

It is very important to sound a cautionary note when thinking about differentiation and in particular we need to be very careful in applying the concept of difference to learners. All learners are, of course, unique and different, as discussed above; this can be seen as a simple fact of life. Many professionals understand this and have moved on in their thinking but in reality labelling is still alive and well and remains an integral part of our education system.

This can be seen clearly if we consider the curricular framework created through the 5–14 development programmes and the Higher Still programme. It is quite common to hear a young person described as a level A pupil, a Foundation pupil, an Access level pupil and so on, and we must be aware that if we do not take great care this can have a damaging effect on these learners. In particular it can have a considerable negative impact on the already fragile self-esteem of vulnerable young people.

However, we live in a society where labelling individuals is an inherent part of life, and all the curricular frameworks we have adopted in Scotland continue to place young people firmly within a hierarchy. The intention is, of course, to create a system where all young people are equally valued and have their potential recognised, but in reality a strong case could be made that what we now have is a system which justifies the separation of children, based on attainment. A system of labelling and stereotyping young people still operates within Scottish education. The current system may be seen by many professionals to be a bit more palatable than previous ones, but for the learners involved the ultimate negative effect on them may be the same. It is those with additional support needs who will be found on the bottom rungs of the hierarchical ladder and no matter how we try to justify this in terms of meeting needs we will still be creating colonies of young people within our schools who are labelled as underachievers. However, it is not necessarily the label that causes the problem but the resulting attitudes and expectations that all too often go hand in hand with this kind of approach.

It is very important therefore to clarify what we mean when we use the word 'differentiation'. Traditionally it has been viewed as a narrow concept as opposed to a process applying to all learners. Simpson (1989) presented a definition which conveyed differentiation as a more complex process of identifying the most effective provision to cater for a range of abilities in one classroom, in such a way that individuals need not always study the same things in the same way at the same time. This is undoubtedly a tall order but it emphasises that differentiation is vital to effective teaching and learning, and applies to all pupils regardless of their level of ability. All too often in schools the process of differentiation has come to be seen as applying to existing resources and tasks; this tends to reinforce the difficulties that learners experience. This has also had the effect of distracting teachers from using the differentiation process to raise some crucial questions about what constitutes an appropriate curriculum and how it can be made more accessible at the developmental/planning stages rather than modifying it as an afterthought.

Young people with additional support needs do not automatically require approaches which are radically different. Fundamentally they need what all learners need: a curriculum which is stimulating, motivating, interesting, which takes account of their learning style and provides opportunities to fulfil their potential. There is no doubt that when effective teachers use differentiation to plan and organise their teaching it can be time consuming and involves a considerable amount of effort. Galton, Simon and Croll (1988) discovered that many teachers understood the importance of differentiation but found it a daunting task and tended to revert back to more traditional practices.

Creating integrated services which cater for pupil diversity

Every document or report written since the early 1990s about special educational needs or additional support needs gives priority to promoting interprofessional collaboration as the basis of effective integrated services. In 1994, for example, the SOED report 'Support for Learning – SEN within the 5–14 Programme' emphasised that many professionals have a role to play in ensuring that the needs of young people are addressed holistically. The report also recognised the equal contributions of all professionals involved, and that the effectiveness of their contribution is dissipated unless integrated with that of others. In the same year, the report 'Effective Provision for Special Education Needs' (SOED 1994b) included interprofessional co-operation as one of its ten distinctive features of effective provision (SOEID) and in 1998 'A Manual of Good Practice in Special Educational Needs' devoted Part 2A to exploring 'working together' as one of its key areas.

Multi-disciplinary working was also given prominence in the 'Better Behaviour – Better Learning' report (SEED 2001) which made clear the importance of 'professionals with a range of different expertise being involved in assessing and supporting young people and their families' (p. 46) This theme was also put forward as central to the success of the new community schools initiative, which aims to promote social inclusion, destroy the cycle of deprivation and ensure that every young person fulfils her/his potential. The prospectus published in 1999 to launch this initiative acknowledged that: 'this will require radically new approaches and these integrated approaches will enable action to be taken early to meet the needs of vulnerable children' (p. 5)

Finally, the 'Count Us In' report (SEED 2003) revisited this recurring theme when it highlighted the importance of joined up working involving a range of professionals. The report mentioned different professional groups, such as social workers, teachers, community education workers and the police, and identified shared clarity of purpose as the most significant factor in effective liaison. It is clear therefore that the creation of integrated services is underpinned by effective interprofessional partnership. However, collaborative practice often remains at the level of rhetoric and if it is to be translated into practice some of the underlying barriers need to be addressed openly and honestly.

The first question which needs to be considered is: why collaborate? According to Lacey (2001), the answer to this question is based on common sense. She points out that it is all too easy for any one group of professionals to take a narrow view of a young person's needs and simply focus on those needs they perceive to be their responsibility. The result can be very fragmentary with professionals working with the individual in conflicting ways rather than adopting a holistic approach. Professionals need to collaborate to promote a truly integrated approach where everyone has a holistic overview and all pursue the shared goals in a co-ordinated way.

Many young people with additional support needs have needs which do not relate specifically to the educational context. However, as mentioned earlier, meeting these needs is often the responsibility of the teacher when the individual has a learning or behavioural difficulty that relates to the school environment or the curriculum. In reality, as one would expect, the needs of these young people are diverse and can impact at all levels of their lives, including home, community and school. Thus many of these young people need the support of several professionals, not as an option but as a vital requisite to ensuring they access the full range of services they require. Young people with medical conditions, sensory and/or physical difficulties, social or emotional difficulties, language and communication difficulties, or behavioural difficulties need the support of other professionals as well as teachers. It seems logical to conclude that the more complex the young person's additional support needs are the more likely it is that a range of professionals will need to be involved and work together.

It is, however, easy to emphasise the importance of collaboration and to pay lip service to concepts such as multi-disciplinary working, community schools, inter-agency partnerships and teamwork. Ensuring these things become a reality and impact on the lives of young people can present challenges to the professionals involved. There are some fundamental barriers to interprofessional partnership which must be acknowledged and overcome if collaborative practice is to be effective. Hamill and Boyd (2001) interviewed a range of professionals, including teachers, social workers, educational psychologists, speech therapists and community education workers, and concluded that good collaborative practice can develop only if all professionals share and agree upon some of the basic principles which underpin it. Some of these principles are explored below.

Valuing one another

Several professionals reported that they did not feel equally valued and that they were sometimes perceived by other professional groups as lower down the professional hierarchy. Consequently they saw their input as being devalued, and their role in school as peripheral. If this situation remains unresolved it will have a negative impact on integrated support systems, which depend to a large extent on effective interprofessional partnerships.

Utilising the range of professional skills

No one professional group has all of the skills required to meet the additional support needs (ASN) of young people. Every opportunity must be taken to share skills and expertise but at the same time the unique role of each professional must be recognised and retained. Professional skills are complementary as opposed to interchangeable. Thus effective support systems for young people (ASN) depend on all professionals accepting that progress can only be made if the full range of professional skills is used collectively to benefit the young person.

Merging professional culture

The collaborative process can be hampered by difficulties in reconciling differing professional cultures. When professional cultures clash the young person may not receive the most appropriate support. One example of this emerged in the way teachers and speech and language therapists viewed their professional role. The therapists expressed their role in terms of a medical model which provided the context for the therapeutic service they provided. The teachers, on the other hand, worked to an educational model and gave higher priority to the cognitive dimension. Thus the therapists saw their role as devising individual programmes and advising the teacher on how to implement them. This approach tended to differ quite markedly from the teacher's view that it was the therapist's role to carry out therapeutic programmes with the child on a one-to-one basis.

Meeting need

Professionals undergo different forms of training and it is inevitable that their perspectives in relation to the needs of young people may differ. There is a tendency to prioritise levels of need according to an accepted professional hierarchy. For the social worker a young person's need is for a stable family life, for the educational psychologist it might be the need to develop self-esteem and for the teacher the need to learn to read. All are, of course, vital to the young person. However, professionals need to see that all these perspectives are equally valid and internalise the view that it is the whole child who matters, not the sum of her/his parts. Many of the professionals interviewed felt that all too often the young person is seen to be a problem to be solved by one particular group or another. Inability to reconcile differing perspectives can result in interprofessional frustration and suspicion rather than harmony and respect.

Roles and responsibilities

Difficulties can arise when the context for interprofessional partnership is the school. It is very important to establish clarity in relation to professional roles and responsibilities and to set out guidelines which show how services are organised and co-ordinated. The aim is to identify a key member of the professional team who can assume responsibility for co-ordinating professional services within the school context. He/she should also have a responsibility for monitoring and evaluating the quality of the service provided.

The key to professional partnership is multi-disciplinary staff development which provides opportunities for all professions to come together in an interprofessional forum where ideas and views can be expressed and shared. It is only in such a forum that potential barriers can be aired and the more deep-rooted questions addressed.

Improving standards for all

Raising the attainment of all young people in Scotland is currently high on the educational agenda. Schools are receiving the message loud and clear that education is at the heart of government policy, and raising standards for all is a priority. The principle consistently conveyed in a plethora of government papers and reports is the creation in schools of cultures of achievement where all young people are equally valued and where each individual has the opportunity to reach their full potential. It is within this context that the concept of additional support needs has evolved and it is within this framework that these needs should be addressed. The drive to raise attainment has in the past often bypassed those for whom learning has been difficult, and it is now vital to establish that we have a duty as educators to ensure all young people realise their full potential.

A renewed focus on raising attainment for all emerged in 1995 when SOEID published the report on 'Standards and Quality in Scottish Schools'. This was followed up in 1996 by 'Achievement for All', which set out some recommendations in relation to raising levels of attainment. This theme was further developed in 1997 in the white paper entitled 'Raising the Standard' which outlined the programme of action aimed at modernising the curriculum and improving teaching standards. The debate on standards has consistently emphasised the central role schools play in providing a quality education which provides opportunities for all. This was summed up in 'Achievement for All' which recommended that schools should 'include an examination of standards of attainment in their development plan and set targets for improvement' (p. 33). Thus the whole Scottish education system has been engaged in a process of change, shaped by a a fairly radical vision which emphasised the importance of raising attainment, realising potential, and where educators are responsive to the needs and wishes of the society and individuals they serve.

This focus on standards provided the context for developments in target setting, and schools were encouraged to set realistic but challenging targets for young people as an effective strategy aimed at raising attainment. A target-setting framework was officially launched in 1998 in the paper 'Raising Standards in Schools – Setting Targets'. Clearly, therefore, a developing culture of quality has been the hallmark of Scottish education in recent years and one document which all schools have been encouraged to use as a benchmark of good practice is 'How Good is Our School?' published by SOEID in 1997. It put quality assurance centre stage and said it was 'about establishing an ethos that only the best will do and that by working together we can make significant improvements' (p. 3).

This commitment to raising standards has continued into the twenty-first century and once again is the central theme in the report 'Improving Our Schools – Assessing Children's Educational Needs – The Way Forward' (2001) which puts target setting, quality assurance, standards of attainment and cultures of achievement at the heart of education. It is vitally important to fully appreciate that the concept of additional support needs has evolved within this context of quality assurance, and schools must consider how to meet these needs within the overall context of achievement for all. Schools are now expected to do everything in their power to eradicate underachievement and at the same time create an inclusive culture where the needs of all, including those with additional support needs, are effectively met. These expectations can be viewed as complimentary or conflicting and it is clear that they have the potential to present challenges to schools and teachers. It remains to be seen exactly how schools will ensure that inclusive education and the drive to raise standards co-exist as compatible aims.

Listening to parents and young people

As far back as 1967 the Plowden Report recognised the importance of positive parental attitudes upon educational performance and highlighted the importance of parents and teachers working in partnership. Research evidence has continued to focus upon the crucial role parents play in their child's education and Armstrong (1996) emphasised that partnership implied 'mutual respect, complementary expertise and a willingness to learn from each other' (p. 18). An inclusive school does everything it can to create structures where parents' views can be expressed openly in a positive, supportive atmosphere. However, the building of partnerships depends on mutual commitment to common principles and it is important to ensure that parents have a place in the decision-making process which affects their children. In 1999 the Scottish Executive, in partnership with Enquire (the independent national information and advice service to parents and young people with special educational needs), produced 'A Parents' Guide to Special Educational Needs'. This guide reiterated the concept of parental rights as presented in the Education (Scotland) Act 1980, particularly the right to 'participate in the assessment and decisions about your child's education – information should be made available to you to help you to contribute and your views should be taken into account in any decisions taken' (p. 33). The Education (Additional report of the consultation on the draft additional Support for Learning) Act (Scotland) (2004) also addresses this issue and emphasises that the parents of young people with additional support needs have the right to be involved in their child's education and should have a clear place within the decision-making processes which affect their child.

The rights of all young people is a theme high on the agenda in Scottish education. Article 12 of the United Nations (1989) Convention on the Rights of the Child asserts that the child has the right to express his/her opinion in relation to all matters affecting him/her. This was taken forward in 1995 in the Children (Scotland) Act which made it clear that children have participation rights in the decision-making processes that affect them as individuals. Participation rights have now been extended by the Standards in Schools Scotland etc. Act (2000) to cover rights in relation to school development and education authority plans which impact on the quality of the young person's life.

The rights of both parents and children have now been set firmly within the inclusion agenda, and schools must demonstrate that they are providing opportunities for open, democratic decision making. Hamill and Boyd (2001, 2003) found that many parents of young people with additional support needs did not feel that they were involved in the decision-making process and reported that decisions relating to their children were often taken by professionals whom they saw as remote and who often had second-hand knowledge of their child. One parent expressed this as follows 'I feel others that I don't really know are making decisions which affect me and my child. My involvement is only a token gesture – no one really listens to me'. Hamill and Boyd also found that some young people felt that the theory of equality did not always translate into practice in schools. Again this is best expressed by an S4 pupil who was a member of her school council: 'Everyone in this school is not treated equally it depends on who you are and who the teacher is.' There is of course a considerable amount of evidence to suggest that most schools do all they can to respect the views of parents and pupils. But there is still room for improvement in some schools where some professionals still find it difficult to address the implications resulting from the move towards a stronger focus on parental and pupil rights.

Commitment to inclusiveness

The ethos within a school conveys the extent to which all individuals are valued and sets the climate for learning. If all young people are to prosper then our schools must pay careful attention to developing an inclusive ethos. We have already devoted a chapter to achieving inclusion in Scottish schools, which looked at some of the criteria that denote an inclusive teacher, so in this section we will simply look at some of the criteria that might be used by a school to audit its commitment to inclusiveness. These have been adapted from work done by Hamill and Boyd.

Table 4.2 Characteristics of inclusive school cultures

• Parents, pupils and staff all feel valued.
• There are high expectations for all pupils.
• The atmosphere in the school is welcoming.
• There are opportunities for all pupils to succeed, and this is celebrated.
• All pupils have the opportunity to participate in social and curricular activities.
• Every effort is made to minimise discriminatory practice.
• Young people are known by staff and treated as individuals.

- External agencies make a positive contribution to the school.
- The style of management is open and receptive.
- Diversity is welcomed and all are treated equally.
- Pupils have an appropriate degree of responsibility for their own learning.
- Stereotyping and labelling individuals is avoided.
- Appropriate support is provided for pupils with additional support needs.
- Resources are distributed fairly.
- The curriculum is designed to include all.
- The school environment is conducive to learning.
- Staff, pupils and parents share the same vision for the school.
- Raising attainment for all is a key priority.
- Staff feel a sense of ownership in relation to school policies.
- Adequate and appropriate CPD opportunities are in place for all staff.

These are some of the criteria which need to be considered if a school is to demonstrate its commitment to inclusion. In relation to each criterion a school needs to ask the question 'What is the evidence to suggest that this criterion has been achieved?'

In this chapter we have looked at some of the basic principles that underpin good practice in supporting young people with additional support needs, regardless of the context in which they are taught. In the following chapters we move on to consider how these principles translate into practice; within mainstream schools and within specialist provision.

SUMMARY

The report, 'Moving Forward! Additional Support for Learning' (2003a) sets out some key principles which underpin good practice in addressing additional support needs. These principles set the climate for learning, and effective schools give them priority in their development planning for the additional needs of their pupils.

These principles are seen to be translated into practice when schools:

- utilise the process of differentiation to cater for a diverse range of needs and to ensure the curriculum is appropriate and accessible to all learners
- emphasise the importance of collaborative teamwork which promotes interprofessional partnerships and the need to take a holistic approach to addressing needs
- ensure that the drive towards raising standards is relevant to all learners and takes full account of those with additional support needs
- listen to and take on board the views of all parents and young people ensuring that they feel their contribution is valued
- demonstrate that every effort is being made to translate the principles underpinning inclusion into practice.

Schools that are able to produce evidence that they are striving to attain all of the above will have established a learning environment which embraces the five principles outlined in this chapter.

POINTS FOR REFLECTION

1 Primary and soecial schools are often described as child-centred and secondar schools are subject-centred. Do you agree or disagree with this distinction?

2 Effective interprofessional partnership is very much dependent on the extent to which all professionals are equally valued. From your own experience do you think that this principle underpins interprofessional collaboration?

3 Do genuine opportunities exist in schools for parents and young people to express their views openly? Do you think parents and young people would agree that their voices are heard and listened to?

5 Additional support needs: pre-school

> I see the mind of a five year old as a volcano
> with two vents: destructive and creative.
>
> **Sylvia Ashton Warner**

Introduction

The pre-school stage was identified in the Warnock Report (DES 1978) as an 'area of first priority' (p. 336). The report recommended that there should be an expansion of provision at this stage for children who at that time were referred to as having special educational needs (SEN) but who are now considered as having additional support needs (ASN). Steady growth in pre-school provision for children with such needs followed the Education (Scotland) Act (1980) and its subsequent amendments. Demand for places in pre-school provision far outweighed supply, and education authorities steadily increased their provision both by creating more education authority-run nursery schools and classes and by establishing childcare partnerships with the private sector.

The Children Act (1989) heightened the focus on the educational aspect of pre-school provision in the UK but until 1994 there was little curricular guidance for staff working in this sector in Scotland. In addition, not all pre-school children had access to pre-school provision. This changed when SOED (1994a) published a report which focused on children under five in Scotland. This report defined the curriculum and identified good practice. This was then used to create a curriculum framework (SOEID 1997) for children in their pre-school year. These guidelines were then extended (SOEID 1999) to include three year olds, and now all children in Scotland, including those with additional support needs, are entitled to a place in pre-school provision and to pre-school education in line with the framework guidelines.

Models of pre-school provision

In Scotland, pre-school children attend one of the following:

- a nursery school (a nursery school in its own right with its own head of establishment)
- a nursery class (set within a primary school, run by a nursery teacher, and with responsibility for management resting with the headteacher of the school)
- a community nursery school (a nursery school in its own right but with an extended clientele (0–4+) and extended day – sometimes this provision is open all year round, and it may also offer after-school care; such a nursery has its own head of establishment who may not always be a teacher but who will employ teachers)
- a playgroup which is part of a childcare partnership with the local authority (an establishment which follows the 3–5 guidelines in the same way as the other provision and which has its own head of establishment who may not always be a teacher but who will employ a teacher)
- a special nursery school (caters exclusively for children who have what in the past have been referred to as severe and complex learning difficulties); such special nursery schools are still provided within some authorities in Scotland and they have their own head of establishment.

As explained in the introduction to this chapter all children in Scotland are entitled to pre-school education and may attend nursery from the age of three. All education authorities' approved pre-school provision follows the SOEID (1999) '3–5 Curriculum Guidelines'.

The principles which underpin good early years practice

The Start Right Report (Ball 1994) presented the findings of a review of the nature of good early years practice and concluded that there are twelve fundamental principles on which this is grounded. These principles are as follows:

- Early childhood is the foundation on which children build the rest of their lives but it is not just a preparation for adolescence and adulthood; it has an importance in itself.

- Children develop at different rates and in different ways – emotionally, intellectually, morally, socially, physically and spiritually. All are important, each is interwoven with others.
- All children have abilities which can (and should) be identified and promoted.
- Young children learn from everything that happens to them and around them.
- Children learn most efficiently through actions rather than instructions.
- Children learn best when they are actively involved and interested.
- Children who feel confident in themselves and their own ability have a head start to learning.
- Children need time and space to produce work of quality and depth.
- What children can do is the starting point of their learning.
- Play and conversation are the main ways in which young children learn about themselves, other people and the world around them.
- Children who are encouraged to think for themselves are more likely to act independently.
- The relationships which children make with other children and with adults are of central importance to their development.

These principles highlight that the needs of young children are complex and interrelated. In assessing young children's needs it is important to ensure that all aspects of a child's development are covered within that assessment. Five dimensions of learning were identified by Barrs (1990). These dimensions overlap and support each other. They are:

- confidence, independence and interest
- experience
- knowledge, skills and understanding
- strategies
- reflectiveness.

All five dimensions form part of a child's life as a learner. These principles and dimensions have been taken into account in the curriculum guidelines that have been devised for children at the pre-school stage.

The aims for early education at the pre-school stage

SOED (1994a) identified the aims for early education at the pre-school stage. SOEID (1997) restated these and emphasised that achieving the stated aims would involve more than merely organising resources for learning. Staff in pre-school settings would be required to consider values, attitudes and the quality of relationships between staff, children, parents and the community. Staff should have positive values about:

- the individual child;
- equal opportunities and social justice;
- partnership with parents/carers;
- the importance of the community;
- education as a life-long process.

Clearly the pre-school stage lays the foundation for life-long learning and is about preparing children to be members of an inclusive society. The aims for pre-school education as stated in SOEID (1997, p. 9) are to:

- provide a safe and stimulating environment, in which children could feel happy and secure
- encourage the emotional, social, physical, creative and intellectual development of children
- promote the welfare of children
- encourage positive attitudes to self and others and develop confidence and self-esteem
- create opportunities for play
- encourage children to explore, appreciate and respect their environment
- provide opportunities to stimulate interest and imagination
- extend the children's abilities to communicate ideas and feelings in a variety of ways.

Children's development and learning are the focus of the 3–5 curriculum guidelines and, in enabling children to make the necessary progress in these areas, staff have a clear focus on the aims for pre-school education.

The pre-school curriculum

The 3–5 Curriculum Guidelines (SOEID 1999) identify five areas of the pre-school curriculum:

- Communication and Language
- Emotional, Personal and Social Development
- Knowledge and Understanding of the World
- Physical Development and Movement
- Expressive and Aesthetic Experience.

These curriculum areas map on to the 5–14 Curriculum as shown in Table 5.1.

Table 5.1 3–5 curriculum areas and their relationship to the 5–14 curriculum

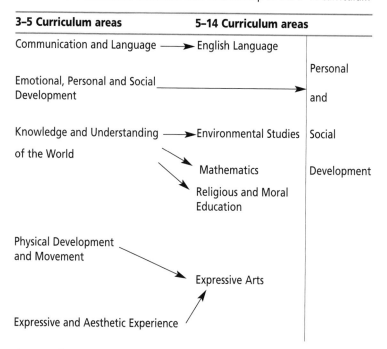

As can be seen in Table 5.1, Emotional, Personal and Social Development is a key curriculum area in the 3–5 Guidelines but is a permeating strand in the 5–14 Curriculum Guidelines rather than a curriculum area in its own right. The area of Physical Development and Movement in the 3–5 guidelines is a subsection of Expressive Arts in the 5–14 Curriculum Guidelines.

Knowledge and Understanding of the World branches out in the 5–14 Curriculum Guidelines to become the three areas of Environmental Studies, Mathematics and Religious and Moral Education. These differences can be accounted for by thinking more about the developing child who enters the nursery, who is still developing language, experience, self-expression, independence, physical movement and a myriad set of concepts and skills which relate to these aspects and to making sense of the world around them: the world of home, nursery and other environments. They are at the start of the big adventure that is education.

Identification of additional support needs

It has been well documented since the 1980 legislation, including SOED (1994a), SOED (1994b) and SOEID (1998), that early identification and early assessment of children's learning needs is crucial to the process of ensuring that children are supported to reach their full potential.

The pre-school stage of identification and assessment produced the effective Pre-School Community Assessment Team (Pre-SCAT) model, which was very successful in ensuring that staff in education, health and social work, and parents, were brought together both in relation to the assessment process itself and in the decision-making process about placement of the child and levels of recommended support and intervention. In a sense this could be viewed as being a pre-emptive step in the form of intervention before children are allowed to fail in their learning. Frank, open discussions among a range of professionals and parents ensure a democratic system of decision making based on a holistic model of assessment. The Pre-SCAT model is represented in Table 5.2.

Table 5.2 The Pre-SCAT Model

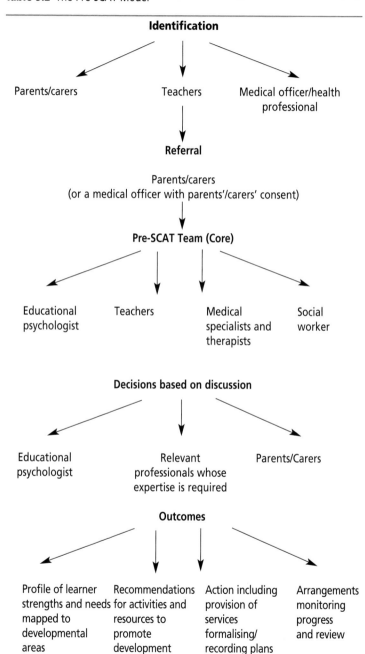

Steps in identifying and assessing a child's additional support needs were stated clearly in SOED (1994b) and SOEID (1998). This came to be known in various authorities as the stepped or staged process of identification and/or assessment and intervention. Following the approval of the Education (Additional Support for Learning) (Scotland) Act 2004 new detailed guidance on the process of identification and assessment will be issued by the Scottish Executive. The report 'For Scotland's Children' (Scottish Executive 2001) recommended setting up a consistent framework for assessing children's needs and sharing information across a range of agencies, including education, health and social care. The Scottish Executive is working with local authorities and health boards to develop such an integrated framework which will apply not only to the pre-school stage but across all ages when identification of support needs takes place. (Scottish Executive 2003).

Early intervention

Since 1997, which saw the launch of the Early Intervention Initiative in Scotland, schools and authorities have been developing early intervention programmes and strategies. Several of these initiatives have involved a careful look at the pre-school stage in an attempt to identify needs at the earliest possible juncture. The intervention in the learning process takes place to help young children make progress in their development before they begin to fail in the formal process of learning. This could be described as the prevention model of intervention. Once children have already failed in the learning process, intervention is of a different kind and could be described as the second chance model.

Of the two models, the former has more appeal; the philosophy which underpins this has its roots in the work of Vygotsky (1962) and Bruner (1983) who believed in supporting children to reach the next level of development rather than waiting for them to progress without assistance. The second chance model will also be required as not all children's needs are apparent at the pre-school stage but, once failure has been experienced, children often develop poor self-esteem, which means the process of second chance intervention can be more difficult. The pre-school stage is therefore a critical identification stage for early intervention.

A number of education authorities in Scotland have introduced screening checks at the pre-school stage for all children, to observe and identify children whose development in some pre-school curricular areas appears to be delayed. Observation techniques in pre-school have developed from the work of Sylva, Roy and Painter (1980). Children are not identified at this stage as having any particular set of difficulties but rather as being at risk of failing in some aspects of their learning. The screening check then becomes the classroom record of the observations that have been made. This together with information from parents, and examples of children's work, informs the plan of what needs to be specifically taught through structured play and activities to cater for class, group and individual needs. This record and planner is reviewed regularly with parents and all professionals who are involved with the child and is used as the basis of the profile which is passed on to and discussed with the primary 1 teacher at the transition stage. Table 5.3 provides an extract from a section of a possible screening checklist for the curriculum area of Physical Development and Movement.

Table 5.3 Screening: observational checklist:
Curriculum area: Physical Development and Movement

Name: John H	Dates	Good	Some difficulties	Marked difficulties	Comments
Balance when seated	18/11/04		✓		Falls off chair on occasions
Balance when standing	18/11/04	✓			Not confident
Balance when walking	18/11/04		✓		Bumps into objects, not confident
Balance when running	18/11/04			✓	Trips up and falls over, looks floppy
Hopping on left foot	18/11/04			✓	Can't balance
Hopping on right foot	18/11/04			✓	Can't balance
Walks up steps (one foot on each step)	18/11/04			✓	Two feet to each step
Walks down steps (one foot on each step)	18/11/04			✓	Needs to hold rail
Catching a ball (two hands)	25/11/04		✓		Doesn't track the ball
Catching a ball (one hand)	25/11/04		✓		Didn't ask him to do this (too difficult)
Throwing a ball (two hands)	25/11/04			✓	Made a reasonable attempt

The noted areas of difficulty on the screening checklist would become the focus of activities to help to improve development, and improvements would be noted on a subsequent occasion. All of the activities, both for screening and development, could take place in the gym hall and more practice could be encouraged at home. If no or very slow improvement was observed then discussion would take place with the parents and a possible referral to the medical officer might be made to rule out the possibility of specific developmental delay in the areas of gross and fine motor skills.

Further observations would be made with regard to this and the other four pre-school curriculum areas of Communication and Language, Personal and Social Development, Knowledge and Understanding of the World, and Expressive and Aesthetic experience. On the basis of the analysis of these observations, plans for intervention and support in the form of an individualised educational programme (IEP) would be drawn up and implemented. Samples of children's drawing and painting and other related work would also be kept as a record of progress.

Personal support plans

In the document 'Moving Forward! Additional Support for Learning' (SEED 2003) pupil support plans are discussed. All children, including those with additional support needs and children at the pre-school stage, from 2003 have a personal learning plan (PLP). This is designed to provide a continuous record and action plan for learning which will begin in pre-school and be maintained throughout the child's school years. Children who have additional support needs will also have an IEP, as mentioned in the section on early intervention. This IEP will become part of a PLP for these children, ensuring that their learning is child-centred with specific learning outcomes identified to target their support needs.

With the developing use of IEPs for children who require additional support in their learning, including children at the pre-school stage, planning and support will begin in pre-school and continue throughout their school education. This should ensure that the transfer of information from pre-school to school will be utilised to good effect.

Individualised planning for children at the pre-school stage

An IEP should be thought of as being:

* a dynamic response to individual needs
* set within the planning for the group/class
* a programme which provides a balanced set of opportunities and experiences
* inclusive in context
* positive in tone.

An IEP is not a separate programme of work which a child with additional support needs should follow in isolation but rather a plan which addresses individual needs within the plan for the group or the class.

The following is a profile of a learner who has some recognised support needs. He is referred to as Robert (not his real name).

ROBERT: A MINI PROFILE   (November 2004)

Robert is in his pre-school year at Pine Nursery. He has been at the nursery since the beginning of the session. He is a very quiet, shy boy who was very upset on the first day and who did not want his mum to leave. He spent much of the first morning crying.

His mum had explained that Robert was a late baby and has a sister who is now working and living away from home. The family lives in a rural, isolated setting and Robert had not previously had any opportunity to mix with other children or share his toys. His dad works long hours and Robert spends most of his time at home with his mother.

Robert can become very absorbed in play activities but plays on his own. He sometimes finds the noise and rough and tumble in the nursery upsetting. Often he appears not to pay very close attention to his key-worker's instructions or directions. At story time he will not sit attentively like the other children and often wanders off to the play area. His hearing was checked as a precaution but it was found to be normal. He has been observed to listen better in one-to-one situations but he seldom volunteers spoken language. His use and understanding of language appears immature and he appears to be reluctant to speak. In a one-to-one situation he will respond when spoken to but his responses are very limited and mostly one-word utterances.

> To date, he still does not play with the other children despite the fact that some have made attempts to interact with him. He finds new situations upsetting and can become tearful if agitated. He has been referred to psychological services for assessment of his needs, and a speech and language therapist now works with Robert and his teacher to help to extend and develop his language and social interaction.

The main areas of concern for Robert appear to be his emotional, personal and social development and his communication and language. These would become the focus of his IEP, with long-term and short-term targets being devised for him. The following three exemplars show possible long-term and short-term target planning for Robert in the curriculum areas of Emotional, Personal and Social Development, and Communication and Language.

- Exemplar 1: Long-term targets – Emotional, Personal and Social Development; and Communication and Language
- Exemplar 2: Short-term targets – Emotional, Personal and Social Development
- Exemplar 3: Short-term targets – Communication and Language

The planning has been done collaboratively by the headteacher, the nursery nurse who is his key-worker, and the speech and language therapist. The names on the exemplars are fictitious.

Exemplar 1 Long-term targets for Robert

Long-term targets	Session 2004/2005
Name: Robert Hastie	**Compiled by J. Smith, O. Trevor, K. Mullen**

Emotional, Personal and Social Development	Success criteria: By end of session Robert will:
1. Develop confidence, self-esteem and sense of security. 2. Form relationships with peers and adults.	1. Cope with new situations without becoming upset 2. Be accepted into the group and interact with peers and adults. 3. Go to the toilet, wash hands, choose a toy unaided.

Curriculum area: Communication and Language

4. Develop attention and listening skills. 5. Use language at the two/three word level.	4. Listen attentively during play and other activities. 5. Use existing vocabulary to make three-word phrases e.g. 'I want snack.'

Robert's present needs are confined to the curriculum areas of Emotional, Personal and Social Development, and Communication and Language. For this reason, the other pre-5 curriculum areas are not featured here.

Exemplar 2 Short-term targets for Robert (Emotional, Personal and Social Development)

Short-term targets	Session 2004/2005

Name: Robert Hastie	Compiled by J. Smith, O. Trevor, K. Mullen

Curriculum area:	Emotional, Personal and Social Development

Long-term targets	Success criteria
1. Develop confidence, self-esteem and sense of security. 2. Form relationships with peers and adults.	1. Cope with new situations without becoming upset 2. Be accepted into the group and interact with peers and adults. 3. Go to the toilet, wash hands, choose a toy unaided.

Short-term targets and success criteria	Teaching strategies/resources personnel
1. By October Robert will participate in simple, interactive games with a familiar adult.	1. **Strategies**: Games like 'Find the hidden object' explained by the key-worker. Favourite toys used as objects to be hidden. **Resources**: favourite toys **Personnel**: key worker
2. By November Robert will smile at and say hello to familiar adults and peers.	2. **Strategy**: role-play activities on meeting people. **Personnel**: key-worker/peers
3. By Christmas Robert will follow a visual timetable for washing hands before snack time.	3. **Strategies**: demonstration by and support from key-worker. **Resource**: visual timetable **Personnel**: key-worker

Exemplar 3 Short-term targets for Robert (Communication and Language)

Short-term targets	Session 2004/2005

Name: Robert Hastie	Compiled by J. Smith, O. Trevor, K. Mullen

Curriculum area:	**Communication and Language**

Long-term targets	Success criteria
1. Develop attention and listening skills. 2. Use language at the two/three word level.	1. Listen attentively during play and other activities. 2. Use existing vocabulary to make three-word phrases e.g. 'I want snack.'

Short-term targets and success criteria	Teaching strategies/resources personnel
1. By November Robert will follow simple verbal instructions.	1. **Strategies**: Key-worker will ask Robert to collect and bring back an object. Robert will be encouraged to join in games in a small group. **Resources**: small toys/pictures **Personnel**: key-worker/peers
2. By Christmas Robert will use existing vocabulary to make two/three-word phrases in making requests e.g. 'I want snack', 'I need toilet', 'Tickets please' (role-play as ticket collector on train).	2. **Strategy**: Use of daily routine and planned activities to encourage language. Key-worker will demonstrate and encourage Robert to repeat phrases. Speech and language therapist will use same vocabulary. **Resources**: familiar materials/picture cards **Personnel**: key-worker, speech and langauge therapist and peers.

Opportunities to reinforce the learning which is the focus of the target setting in the IEP will arise through the planning for the group/class. Robert's mother would also be encouraged to reinforce the planned activities and language at home.

The following class plan is based on the topic 'Transport and Shape'. The key-worker or teacher has planned this for all children, including Robert, but will also have planned to ensure that Robert's individual needs as outlined in exemplars 1–3 are addressed within the plan.

Class Plan: Transport and Shape

Emotional, Personal and Social Development	Communication and Langauge	Knowledge and Understanding of the World
Turn taking and sharing in the play activities based on transport and shape. (Trip on pretend bus/train/car/aeroplane). Response to activities likes/dislikes. Feelings about what happened in the stories about transport.	Learning vocabulary: triangle, rectangle, square, circle, window, door, wheels, train, boat, car, bus, tickets please. Learning language instructions. Answers to open-ended questions. Learning about books, stories, songs about transport and shape e.g. 'the wheels on the bus' etc.	Recalling trips on transport, what shape is a wheel? Children's ideas and experiences of being on a bus, train, aeroplane, boat, car. Trip to Transport Museum by bus. Talk about fuel to make transport move. Matching by size, shape, colour (cars etc.).

Expressive and Aesthetic Development		Physical Development and Movement
Drama: respond to and create roles, e.g. train driver, ticket collector. Pretend to be an aeroplane with wings moving through the sky. (How does it feel?) Painting of transport.		Respond to action songs (model the action). Climbing up the stairs on the 'bus'. Movement of different transport (pretend).

From the general plan, Robert's teacher could identify emotional, personal and social development targets in line with Robert's IEP. She could ensure that the children have to pretend to meet someone at the bus/train station and to smile and say hello to them. This would include Robert and would help him to meet his short-term target 2. (Emotional, Personal and Social Development). He could be the ticket collector on the train and have to say 'tickets please'. This would help to meet short-term target 2 in the area of Communication and Language. Within this plan there would be lots of opportunities for Robert and others to follow simple verbal instructions which would also help him to attain short-term target 1 in Communication and Language. In this way his teacher can ensure that the IEP is being followed within a shared learning context rather than separately.

Sometimes it will be necessary for Robert to work one-to-one with an adult but most of the time Robert should be working as part of a group so that he can be fully included in the work and socially accepted by his peers.

Emergent literacy and emergent numeracy

In the pre-school stage children are developing their emergent literacy and numeracy. They are not taught literacy and numeracy *per se* but rather the foundation blocks which will help them to make the transition from emergent literacy and emergent numeracy to literacy and numeracy. In the fun activities which are set up in the nursery, children are encouraged to listen to and act out familiar stories which have been introduced by the teacher. This develops and enriches their language and lays the foundation of an understanding of concepts of print. Their phonological awareness is also developed through listening to rhyme and clapping the beats in their own names. They are encouraged to recognise their own and other children's names and to play with plastic letters and make and match letter shapes out of play dough. They learn their colours and match and name these using various objects and toys. They sing counting songs and rhymes.

Further language enrichment and development comes from involvement in imaginative activities which are set within real contexts and which are based on pictures, stories or outings to which the children bring their own experiences. They will play at hospitals and schools in the play corner, use the wendy house as a castle being defended against enemies, have real birthday and tea parties, make cakes, match place settings, build objects with construction blocks. They have pretend telephone conversations with friends and in the process are developing many skills and understanding lots of concepts all of which feed into emergent literacy and numeracy as they are developing their Physical Development and Movement, Communication and Language, Emotional, Personal and Social Development, Knowledge and Understanding of the World and Expressive and Aesthetic Experience.

Children with additional support needs already identified at this stage will require more support and more opportunities for reinforcement to develop the skills and understanding which they will require at this preparatory emergent literacy and numeracy stage to equip them to begin the formal process of learning to read, write, spell and deal with computation once they are in primary school.

Working in partnership with parents and carers

Pre-school settings are good examples of the partnership with parents/carers and families which has been advocated by SOED (1994), SOEID (1998) and the Scottish Executive (2003). It is essential to involve parents/carers and families in the education of children with additional support needs. Parents have the responsibility to ensure that their children receive an education suitable for their age, ability and aptitude. In addition they have the right, within certain limits, to make a placing request for their child to attend the school of their choice. The principles which underpin parental involvement emphasise that parents of children with additional support needs can be involved in their child's education by:

- participating in assessment and review of needs and future needs assessment
- selecting an appropriate school placement
- passing on to teachers relevant information from doctors and other professionals
- suggesting ways which are likely to be effective in learning and teaching

- reinforcing new skills and learning at home and in the community
- supporting school activities
- offering advice and support to other parents of pupils in the school.

A very positive aspect of the pre-school stage is the good practice of partnership with parents/carers displayed within a range of establishments. Most parents/carers are keen to be involved in the pre-school context and in carrying out work with their children at home. There is evidence of very good relationships between staff in pre-school and parents/carers who are welcomed into the pre-school establishments and talk with staff on a daily basis, usually when delivering or collecting their child to or from nursery. In order to capitalise and build on this partnership, materials/tasks are sent home for the parents/carers and their children to work on together.

A good example of this is the use of story sacks which contain a book, a soft toy related to the story in the book and some games which also centre on the storyline or theme. Fun is the common denominator in the materials that are sent home with very clear instructions about how they should be used. There is usually a feedback sheet which goes back to the nursery to let staff know about the child's interest in the task, the language that has been used in the process of doing the task, whether it was easy or a little difficult, etc. This information also adds to the holistic picture which is being built up about the child's progress.

Regular reviews with parents/carers take place. Educational toys and games are often sent home on loan. Parents/carers become involved in making new resources for story sacks and other items. Parents/carers often come into the nursery to spend time with their children in play activities, to provide more one-to-one language exchange within a structured activity. For the child, this is very valuable as the child can see that home and nursery are working together. There are also examples of parents who speak English and another language like Urdu who are invited into the nursery setting to use Urdu to translate a story that the nursery teacher might be telling the children in English but that some Urdu-speaking children, whose English is not very good, might not understand.

Transition

Provided good preparation for the important move to primary school (transition) is made, all children's transition from pre-school to school should be a relatively easy process. However, children with additional support needs will be particularly vulnerable at this stage and will require additional support from adults familiar to them as they make this transition.

Some nursery schools and classes have arrangements with the primary school for classroom assistants from the primary 1 class to spend time in the nursery with the most vulnerable children, getting to know them and vice-versa. This person then becomes the familiar face on entry to the primary school. Similarly some nursery schools and classes send a nursery nurse into primary 1 for some time at the transition stage ensuring that, again, a familiar face is around at the beginning of term.

In all cases when children at the pre-school stage have additional support needs it is always best practice for the nursery teacher to meet with the primary 1 teacher to discuss face to face the individual support needs of children. The paperwork in itself is no substitute for first-hand information.

SUMMARY

Pre-school provision is expanding considerably as we move forward in the twenty-first century. All children have an entitlement to a place in pre-school. Curriculum guidelines are in place to ensure that children's development in important areas is targeted. Early intervention initiatives have introduced screening programmes which identify children's strengths and support needs at this critical stage. A real opportunity is therefore created to take preventative steps to support children's learning and reduce the risks of failure. IEPs are introduced at this stage to ensure continuity of support and planning, and partnership with parents is at the heart of the pre-school's responses to children's needs. The emphasis on the importance of transition stages also applies to pre-school. Preparation steps for this critical phase should be taken in partnership by both the pre-school setting and the primary school.

POINTS FOR REFLECTION

1 Do all staff in pre-school settings have the opportunity to undertake professional development with an emphasis on child development?

2 What preventative steps are taken in pre-school settings to support learning and reduce the risk of failure, so that a solid learning foundation is laid?

3 How much planning and preparation for transfer to primary school is in place in pre-school settings to ensure the transition process is smooth? Do the primary school staff share in this process as part of a partnership?

6 Additional support needs: primary school

> What greater gift can we offer the republic than to teach and instruct our young.
>
> Cicero

Introduction

Before the publication of the HMI progress report (SED 1978), mainstream primary school support for pupils who were at that time categorised as being in need of remedial help was provided to individuals or to small groups two or three times a week by a remedial teacher. The Primary Memorandum of 1965, with its emphasis on an education suited to a pupil's 'age, aptitude and ability', had advocated mixed-ability classes in Scottish primary schools. For pupils who required remedial help following screening checks on reading, phonics and number at the end of Primary 2, remedial teachers drew up individual work programmes largely for reading, phonics, spelling, number work and related activities. Remedial teachers were trained in diagnostic assessment and would pinpoint weak aspects of pupils' cognitive development. Remedial programmes would therefore, in addition to the basics, address cognitive developmental weaknesses like auditory sequential memory or visual discrimination, and remedial teaching time would provide additional practice in developing these individual aspects.

The individual work programmes which were created by remedial teachers would cover work that the pupils were expected to do during class time and which the remedial teacher would check over when pupils next visited the remedial teacher's room. The reality of such practice determined that "remedial" pupils were isolated from the class when they went for tuition provided by the remedial teacher. Class teachers and sometimes headteachers appeared to misinterpret roles and responsibilities so that if pupils were seen by the remedial teacher the class teacher assumed that the responsibility for such pupils' learning was the remedial teacher's since the pupil was on the remedial teacher's list. Sadly, completion of work programmes was dependent on the class teacher ensuring that the work was done and facilitating the provision of time in class for pupils to carry it out. Often, the pupil would be required to do the work of the class/group first and then, if there was time, he/she could do the work for the remedial teacher. Bizarrely such pupils could have two reading books – one from the class teacher (which was often too difficult) and one at a more appropriate level from the remedial teacher. Remedial time often replaced time for music, PE or art and so these pupils experienced a narrow curriculum and a heavier workload (the group work and remedial work). It was almost as if they were being punished for not being able to learn easily. Being taught by the remedial teacher in isolation of the class created a stigma and these pupils at that time came to be referred to by their peers, and sometimes their teachers, as at best "remedial pupils".

Often pupils who worked with the remedial teacher, when considered to have improved sufficiently in their reading, spelling or number work, would be discharged back to their class group but unless cognisance of the class progress was taken into account, in reality, this was a discharge back to the "bottom group" because the other pupils had often improved to a greater degree in the interim. Where remedial support was at a premium, some pupils might have help from P3 to P6 but might not be provided with such help in P7 as priority was then given to the new P3s.

The system was clearly fundamentally flawed and ready for change. Such change was advocated in the HMI progress report of 1978 which criticised remedial provision of the time and turned the spotlight on the curriculum as the major source of pupils' difficulty with learning. This report marked a sea change in respect of curriculum-related barriers to learning and introduced new ways of working for support teachers. It also led ultimately to the creation of the 5–14 Curriculum Guidelines introduced in 1991, which continue to inform curriculum planning within primary schools at the present time.

Primary school provision

All primary schools, regardless of size and location, follow the 5–14 Curriculum Guidelines. These guidelines provide a framework of curriculum planning for all pupils. Every pupil, whether or not they have additional support needs, is expected to be on the 5–14 curriculum planning map. For some pupils, their needs determine that they require different access routes to the curriculum and therefore to the learning process but the aims for all children must be the same. Responsibility for all pupils' learning rests squarely on the shoulders of class teachers and the whole school. Where support for learning teachers are involved with identified pupils, their role is not solely about supporting pupils but extends to supporting teachers, advising management, working alongside class teachers in co-operative teaching sessions, liaising with parents and other professionals who are involved with individual pupils, and leading staff development sessions on aspects of support for learning or additional support needs. Each primary school is expected to have a support for learning co-ordinator, who has management responsibility for ensuring that a streamlined whole-school approach to meeting needs is in place and is fully understood by, and communicated to, all staff. Some primary schools have a designated in-house support for learning teacher who is appointed full or part-time to the school. Others may have visiting specialist support teachers from a network team or cluster whose line manager may be a network co-ordinator. All primary schools will have some additional support time allocated to them in their pursuit of enabling all pupils to reach their potential. The present model of support provision is markedly different from the pre-1978 model, not only in its form but also in the philosophy that underpins it. Tables 6.1 and 6.2 clarify these differences.

Table 6.1 Pre-1978 remedial provision model

		Philosophy	Results
Identification?	End of P2 via reading and number standardised tests	Some children not ready to learn before age 7. We play the waiting game.	Children experience failure ↓ damaged self-esteem
Support (remedial teacher) whom?	Bottom group pupils (based on performance in standardised tests)	Selection on performance in comparision with peers.	More damage to self-esteem
When and frequency?	P3–P6 (discontinued in P7 if not enough remedial teacher time) 2 or 3 X ½ hours a week in small groups or sometimes one-to-one.	Skill them up to return to class group. Can't be sustained long-term.	Some discharged but often still not as well progressed as peers so still in the bottom group. Others left without help (had their turn and their quota).
Where?	Extracted from class	Good for concentration. Shifts responsibilities from class teacher to remedial teacher.	Miss class work so fall further behind in other areas. Stigmatised (going to remedial). Class teacher no longer responisble.
What?	Reading, phonics, spelling, number as necessary, and cognitive developmental skills areas. Individual work programme[a]	Target areas of weakness.	Focus on basic skills, improved levels but often duplicated effort. Improved skills not always transferred to reading etc.

[a]Not an individualised educational programme or IEP. This programme was one of separate/different work which was done by the individual largely in isolation from the group.

Table 6.2 'Support for learning' provision model

		Philosophy	Results
Identification?	Earliest possible juncture but at any time when difficulties arise (strengths and weaknesses). (Pre-school to P7) screening checks based on criterion-referenced assessment and referral by parent, support for learning teacher, co-ordinator or class teacher.	Earliest possible identification so ensuring earliest intervention. Rolling programme of identification so none slip through the net.	Avoid experience of failure which can result in poor self-esteem. Early intervention possible, catch all who are at risk.
Support (support specialist and class teacher, in partnership with parents and other professionals) whom?	All who are identified as being at risk.	We don't wait for children to become ready. We support them in their learning as soon as possible. Whole-school responsibility and collaboration in the process by a range of professionals and parents.	Experience of failure does not become the norm.
When? Frequency?	P1–P7 as required but usually within the planning for the group or the class if possible and some essential individualised support.	Target support needs. In class, support through reducing barriers to learning	Whole-school. systems and strategies. More appropriate education. No cut-off point for support.
Where?	In-class whenever possible and desirable.	Pupils experience the breadth of the curriculum. No gaps in teaching and learning opportunites.	Fully included member of the class/group.
What?	Any aspect of learning which is problematic. Differentiated approaches and strategies.	Use strengths to overcome difficulties in learing. Match teaching styles to learning styles. Overcome barriers to learning.	Appropriate education. Fewer barriers in the way of pupils reaching their potential.

The primary school curriculum

The 5–14 Curriculum Guidelines identify five key areas of the primary school curriculum:

- English Language
- Mathematics
- Environmental Studies
- Religious and Moral Education
- Expressive Arts.

Personal and Social Development is also important within the 5–14 Curriculum framework and is a permeating strand or cross-curriculum aspect (Scottish Executive Education Department 2000) which sits alongside Religious and Moral Education together with Health Education. The other cross-curriculum aspects are education for work, education for citizenship, the culture of Scotland, information and communication technology. SED (1978, paragraphs 4.6 to 4.9) laid down some markers for the curriculum, which included:

- curriculum aims should be the same for all pupils
- pupils should not all have to study the same things at the same pace, in the same way
- objectives for pupils should take into account their age, aptitude and ability
- the curriculum must sustain skill and interest and get pupils across the plateau of learning
- demands on pupils for higher skill and interest must be not only appropriate but also sufficiently challenging
- de-contextualised activity, such as routine drilling, should be avoided
- reducing or dropping aspects of the curriculum for individual pupils who require greater provision for the development of basic skills should not be at the expense of enjoyable or creative activities, or those which offer experience of success.

These markers are central to the principle of education for all, with differentiation serving as the route which makes this an attainable goal.

Each curriculum area is divided into attainment outcomes and strands. There are also attainment targets. Sometimes it will be necessary, depending on the nature of some pupils' additional support needs, to omit some strands or create new strands and smaller, more attainable targets. The curriculum guidelines present a framework; they are not designed to be restrictive. For example, if we consider the attainment outcome of 'writing' with its strand on 'handwriting', for a pupil who has dyspraxia and finds the fine motor skill of handwriting very difficult or in some cases impossible, the handwriting strand would become, for example, 'handwriting and written reporting using ICT'. Handwriting would continue to be taught but ICT skills would be introduced to reduce the pressure on the volume of the handwritten work. Detailed consideration of such issues is reported in SOED (1995). There is a flexibility factor of 20% within the guidelines, which were updated in 2000 to ensure better balance according to individual needs.

Identification of additional support needs in the primary school

Identification of needs is a process of continuous assessment not only of learning needs but of additional needs which may arise as a result of pupils' changing circumstances. Primary schools and staff must be vigilant in their duty to identify factors which impact on pupils' learning. Social or other circumstances should be known to the school and monitored but may only become concerns if there is evidence of problems impacting on self-esteem and/or the learning process for that pupil. The new legislation (Scottish Parliament 2004) supports the ideal that education is child-centred. Each pupil's additional support needs should be considered in the light of individual circumstances.

Normally where there are marked additional support needs arising from specific barriers to a pupil's learning these will have been identified at the pre-school stage and as a result of screening information about the individual pupil's needs will have been passed to the primary school when the pupil transfers. However, not all additional support needs will be recognisable at the pre-school stage so screening in P1 is also considered to be crucial. Like the pre-school screening discussed in the previous chapter, P1 screening may also focus on developmental skills but will also identify where pupils are in relation to progress in literacy and numeracy development.

Table 6.3 Progress in reading: Screening profile

Name of pupil: Charles Smith (fictitious name) Date of birth: 10.4.99 Class: P1		Date of assessment: 25.10.04
Concepts of print	**Recognises/ understands**	**Fails to recognise/ misunderstands**
Points to title of book	✓	
Points to name of author	✓	
Points to picture	✓	
Points to where we begin story	✓	
Show a letter (using 2 strips of card)		showed a word
Show a word (using 2 strips of card)		showed a letter
Discrimination		
Letters/sounds	a, c, e, f, g, h, i, k, l, m, o, r, s, t, v, x	b, d (mixed these up), j, n, p, q, u, w, y, z (didn't know these)
Words/letters sort		
Sort cards: some letters; some words		put words together but called them letters and vice versa
Look and say words from reading book	a, his, to, my, mum, see, school, the	boy, dog (said dog, boy), went, and

Table 6.3 is an extract from a P1 screening checklist about progress in reading. It provides clear pointers about gaps in reading development. These would then become the individual targets for planning the next steps in reading development for Charles (fictitious name).

Teachers' observations are also important as an assessment tool and provide the formative assessment information which can be used for planning next steps. If a pupil has found a new concept difficult, then this can be noted and further explanation can be provided on a subsequent occasion as part of a working plan. By listening to pupils, teachers can quickly tune-in to misunderstandings or shaky concepts and clarify things for the pupil at that time. Regular checks on pupils' learning should become part of the teaching and learning routine.

Assessment is therefore multi-faceted. It can be a blanket screening check as in P1, formative feedback by pupils and observations by teachers, and summative in the form of learning checks which can take place at regular intervals. All concerns should be noted and where there is obvious lack of progress, this should be discussed with the support for learning co-ordinator. In consultation with the support for learning specialist teacher some adjustments to the planned work may be made for a pupil and parents consulted. Plans will be reviewed and if problems continue and parents agree, a referral may then be made to other support services to provide another layer of support and advice for the pupil and the teacher. These actions follow the stepped or staged process of identification/assessment and referral outlined in SOED (1994) and SOEID (1998a).

National priorities in education: primary schools

The Scottish Executive (2002) launched support materials for the national priorities in education. Education authorities are charged with a key role in driving these priorities forward. Schools are expected to undergo a process of self-evaluation based on quality indicators via the "How Good is Our School" pack (Scottish Executive 2002). Education authorities will agree national priority targets with schools as a result of moderation of the process of self-evaluation. To streamline the process, each authority is expected to have a National Priorities Co-ordinator. The national priorities are outlined in Table 6.4.

Table 6.4 National priorities

Priorities	Explanation of priorities
1. Achievement and Attainment	To raise standards of educational attainment for all in schools, especially in the core skills of literacy and numeracy and to achieve better levels in national measures of achievement including examination levels.
2. Framework for Learning	To support and develop the skills of teachers, the self-discipline of pupils and to enhance school environments so that they are conducive to teaching and learning.
3. Inclusion and Equality	To promote equality and help every pupil benefit from education, with particular regard to pupils with disabilities and special educational needs (now additional support needs) and to Gaelic and other lesser-used languages.
4. Values and Citizenship	To work with parents, to teach pupils respect for staff and one another and their interdependence with other members of their neighbourhood and society and to teach them the duties and responsibilities of citizenship in a democratic society.
5. Learning for Life	To equip pupils with the foundation skills, attitudes and expectations necessary to prosper in a changing society and to encourage creativity and ambition.

(Scottish Executive 2002) Summary Table

Early intervention initiative and intervention to support learner needs

In Chapter 5 the early intervention initiative which was actioned in Scotland in 1997 was discussed in relation to the pre-school setting. The early intervention initiative did not only target pre-school but was also concerned with the education of pupils from pre-school to P2. Primarily the initiative was concerned with raising levels of literacy and numeracy and so wide research into strategies which could improve these core skills areas was undertaken by education authorities across Scotland who were involved in the funded initiative. National priorities 1 and 4, 'Achievement and Attainment' and 'Learning for Life' (mentioned above), share this goal.

Important lessons about effective teaching approaches have been learned as a result of this national focus which was monitored and evaluated by authorities and HMI. Some of the successful strategies which were favoured include:

- developing pupils' phonological awareness
- fun approaches to the teaching of phonics
- realistic pacing of learning
- multi-sensory approaches to teaching and learning which target pupils' learning styles
- high but realistic expectations for all pupils
- establishing the links between reading, writing, listening and talking
- metacognition or thinking about thinking
- higher-order reading skills like prediction, introduced at the beginning of the process of learning to read
- links being made across different aspects of learning to provide reinforcement and consolidation
- involving parents and keeping them informed of their child's progress
- recording progress and using records to inform next steps in planning
- passing on and communication of records of progress from teacher to teacher
- more partnership with other professionals.

Such strategies are known to be effective, and teachers at the P1 and P2 stages who utilise these approaches in their classrooms are likely to be effective teachers. What we should not lose sight of is the fact that the early intervention initiative was about finding appropriate methods to improve general standards of literacy and numeracy. Despite effective teaching approaches, some children still fail to learn, or struggle to learn. When this happens, intervention in the form of support for their learning should be put in place.

Class teachers must be vigilant in their continuous assessment of pupils' progress to recognise when a pupil is failing and if, despite support from the class teacher, such lack of progress continues, referral to the support for learning co-ordinator should take place at this point. We no longer wait for children to become more mature in the hope that they will then magically be more switched on to learning. This is unlikely to happen. We must intervene in the learning process to ascertain what their individual learning needs are and target teaching to take account of these. The earliest possible intervention is strongly advocated. Referral of this nature could be at any point within the primary school and not exclusively at P1 or P2. Pupils can have difficulty at any stage on the learning continuum.

Individualised planning for primary pupils

Pupils who have additional learning support needs, where such needs are centred on learning, will have an individualised educational programme in addition to a personal learning plan. Individualisation in the learning process does not mean that pupils will work individually on all or some aspects of their learning; it simply means that account will be taken of their individual needs when planning the work of the class or the group.

Table 6.3 highlights some of the gaps in a pupil's (Charles's) reading progress and development. These are Charles's individual needs within the teaching of reading. They could be catered for quite easily by involving Charles, along with others in Charles's group, in some revision work on concepts of print, letter/sound correspondence, letter recognition and 'look and say' vocabulary. The teacher or classroom assistant could work with Charles's group to reinforce these aspects on different occasions. Charles's parents/carers could also be encouraged to carry out explained tasks at home to further reinforce these weak areas. Some board, card and/or computer games incorporating the vocabulary or the letters to be learned could be created for Charles as further reinforcement for work at home or with a partner in class.

In this way, Charles's needs are being targeted, but Charles is not being segregated from his group or being made to feel different. If progress continued to be elusive then his class teacher would seek further advice from the support for learning co-ordinator and/or the support for learning specialist. The needs of pupils at any stage in the primary school can be addressed in this way. The basic formula for checking on progress is as follows:

- regular check on progress (assess)
- identify gaps/difficult concepts (support needs)
- make a record and plan for individual needs (set targets)
- teach again or revise as required (adapt plan/targets to suit needs)
- reinforce/consolidate learning within a shared learning context whenever possible; involve parents/buddies as required; remember that games/computers add an element of fun and motivation to the learning process (additional reinforcement)
- check again on progress.

Charles's case is fairly straightforward, some pupils' additional support needs are more complicated. Consider the following profile of Marie, a (fictitious) P5 pupil whose needs are much more marked.

MARIE: A MINI PROFILE   (October 2004)

Marie is in P5 at Knowepark Primary school. She transferred to Knowepark in P3 when her family moved into the area. At that time she appeared to be coping with the demands of school although it took her some time to settle in and to make friends. The teachers did notice that she was a little unco-ordinated at that time. Marie is tall for her age and is a bit clumsy. She bumps into other children, who find this very annoying. Most of the girls in the class tend to ignore her although she is friends with one girl who is also a bit of a social isolate in the class.

Marie's handwriting is extremely untidy to the point of being almost illegible. She doesn't seem to be able to improve her fine motor skills in this area and is painfully aware of the difference between her handwriting and the other pupils'. She hasn't yet made the transition from printing to cursive handwriting. This year in P5 she appears to be very easily upset and becomes tearful if her teacher doesn't have nice things to say about her work. Her teacher was very alarmed when Marie announced loudly that she hated PE and refused to go to the class with the other children. Instead she spent this time crying outside the headteacher's office. Her mum has now said that Marie hasn't really been happy since she came to Knowepark and is very worried about the future for her.

Marie: Responding to her additional support needs

There are two main areas of concern for Marie based on this profile. Her poor gross and fine motor control could be the result of dyspraxia, sometimes referred to as developmental co-ordination disorder. Teachers don't always know very much about this, and children like Marie tend to be considered as simply clumsy and untidy. Real social difficulties can result, as in Marie's case, because other children can be intolerant of the behaviours which are the result of poor co-ordination.

Marie is now at an age when she is very aware that she is different and she is not in control of changing her 'clumsiness'. This, added to her awareness of her problems with handwriting, has obviously caused her much distress and damage to self-esteem. In turn this is compounded by the fact that she is lonely and unpopular. Both Marie's personal and social development and her dyspraxia have to be tackled now before any more damage to her self-esteem is incurred.

The support for learning co-ordinator has taken advice from the support for learning specialist teacher who knows a bit about dyspraxia. Marie has been referred with her mum's consent to the occupational therapist (OT) via the school medical officer. The OT has advised that Marie engages in a movement skills programme which can be carried out at home on a daily basis. A daily diary goes home each day and Marie's mum feeds back on Marie's progress in the diary. Marie also works on this programme once a week with the OT who is monitoring Marie's progress. Marie's class teacher is also monitoring her handwriting which she has been told should improve as Marie's gross motor skills improve. In the meantime she is using a lap top computer to word process some of her written work to improve on the presentation. In addition to the motor skills programme, Marie's class teacher is targeting social interaction as part of the class plan. Circle Time has been introduced to help to raise awareness of the need for tolerance and mutual respect. It is still early days but Marie appears to be a bit more happy and her mum has indicated that she has observed an improvement in her motor control.

An IEP for Marie

An individualised educational programme has been drafted for Marie and involved the learning support specialist, the learning support co-ordinator, the inclusion co-ordinator, the headteacher, Marie's mum, her class teacher and the occupational therapist in discussion and planning. Both long-term and short-term targets have been identified in the following three exemplars:

- Exemplar 1: Long-term IEP target
- Exemplar 2: Short-term IEP target
- Exemplar 3: Short-term IEP target.

All names in the exemplars are fictitious.

Exemplar 1 Long-term IEP targets for Marie

Long-term targets	Session 2004/2005 (from October 2004)
Name: Marie Bowman	Compiled by K. Kelly, M. Brown, J. Matheson, S. Palmer, D. Bowman, K. England and L. Scott
Personal and Social Development	**Success Criteria:** **By the end of the session ✓** **Marie will:**
1. Develop confidence and self-esteem.	1. Be happy to participate in activities like PE.
2. Have improved social interaction with her peers.	2. Be more socially included within the class.
3. Present neater written work.	3. Produce legible linked script to attain level C in handwriting and presentation.
Expressive Arts	
4. Develop better co-ordination at the gross motor level.	4. Engage on a daily basis in a movement skills programme.[a]
Reflective/Evaluative Comments	

[a]as recommended by Portwood (2000)

Exemplar 2 Short-term IEP targets for Marie

Short-term targets	Session 2004/2005 (from October 2004)
Name: Marie Bowman	Compiled by K. Kelly, M. Brown, J. Matheson, S. Palmer, D. Bowman, K. England and L. Scott
Curriculum area:	Personal and Social Development Through PE in Expressive Arts

Long-term targets	Success criteria
1. Develop confidence and self-esteem.	1. Be happy to participate in PE.
2. Have improved social interaction with her peers.	2. Be more socially included within the class.
4. Develop better co-ordination at the gross motor level.	4. Engage on a daily basis in a movement skills programme.

Short-term targets and success criteria	Teaching strategies/resources/personnel
1. By Christmas, Marie will participate more confidently in PE activities designed around her movement skills programme.	1. A 'stations' approach to motor skills utilised for all pupils in the class in PE but based on Marie's programme. (Marie and other pupils don't know this.) Programme also to be in the routine at home. **Resources**: benches, bean bags, large ball, daily diary for use between mum and class teacher. **Personnel**: OT, PE teacher, class teacher, Marie's mum.
2. By Christmas, Marie will have been the special person during Circle Time and have received positive feedback from her peers.	2. **Strategies**: Circle Time activities once a week: whole-class positive feedback encouraged for each special person. Feelings and emotions and importance of friendship and tolerance emphasised. **Resources**: Circle Time worksheets and activities. Personnel: class teacher/peers.
4. Engage on a daily basis in a movement skills programme	4. Strategies: Assess gross motor development and continue to observe progress in daily programme. Assess again at Christmas. Programme also to be used at home with mum.

Reflective/Evaluative Comments

Exemplar 3 Short-term IEP targets for Marie

Short-term targets	Session 2004/2005 (from October 2004)
Name: Marie Bowman	Compiled by K. Kelly, M. Brown, J. Matheson, S. Palmer, D. Bowman, K. England and L. Scott
Curriculum area:	English Language (Handwriting and Presentation

Long-term targets	Success criteria
3. Present neater written work.	3. Produce legible linked script to attain Level C in handwriting and presentation.

Short-term targets and success criteria	Teaching strategies/resources/personnel
3. By Christmas, Marie's handwriting will show evidence of better formation of letters and be more legible.	3. **Strategies**: Concentrate on perceptuo-motor skills[a] to develop better hand-eye co-ordination. **Resources**: Marie to work on this at home using worksheets and roll and write materials[b] (homework). In class encourage Marie to remember the formation of letters introduced through the roll and write activities. **Personnel**: class teacher/Marie's mum. Mum to ensure that work-sheets come back to class for marking.

Reflective/Evaluative Comments

[a] Teodorescu and Addy (1996)
[b] Fidge (1994)

Partnership with parents/carers and other professionals

The IEP designed for Marie demonstrates that Marie's mother is being consulted about, and is involved in, her child's education. Such partnership is based on mutual respect for parents' and understanding of parents'/carers' rights in the education of their children. SOEID (1998b) were anxious to enhance the role of parents/carers in school education. The roles and responsibilities of parents are clearly explained by the Scottish Executive Education Department (2003).

Parents/carers must be consulted about any learning needs which the school identifies and, whenever possible, the support which parents can offer should be accessed. Most parents/carers of children at the primary stage are only too happy to be involved. It must be acknowledged, however, that some parents/carers may choose not to be so involved. When this happens, the school must action its duty of care to try to provide the support that children like Marie, who has additional support needs, must have if her needs, which are currently barriers to learning, are to be addressed.

Class teachers must be prepared to work collaboratively with a range of professionals, and planning for pupils should also be a collaborative process. Primary schools must establish links with all services – education, health and social work – to ensure that all avenues of professional support can be accessed when required. Figure 6.1 identifies avenues of support.

Figure 6.1

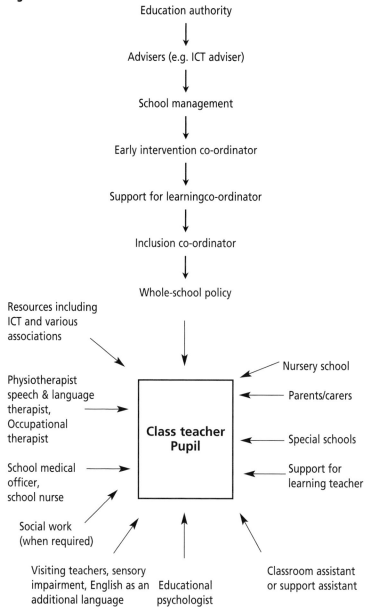

Education authority

Advisers (e.g. ICT adviser)

School management

Early intervention co-ordinator

Support for learningco-ordinator

Inclusion co-ordinator

Whole-school policy

Resources including
ICT and various
associations

Physiotherapist
speech & language
therapist,
Occupational
therapist

School medical
officer,
school nurse

Social work
(when required)

**Class teacher
Pupil**

Nursery school

Parents/carers

Special schools

Support for
learning teacher

Visiting teachers, sensory
impairment, English as an   Educational
additional language   psychologist

Classroom assistant
or support assistant

Information and communication technology (ICT)

Increasingly ICT is being used successfully as part of planned programmes of responding to individual needs. Most education authorities now have an ICT adviser or tutor who will provide advice and resources to schools to cater for specific needs. Where new hardware and software is provided to schools and pupils, it is important that both staff and pupils are trained in its use. The provision of the equipment is not sufficient in itself unless such training and practice is built into the equation.

Transition

The transition from primary 7 to secondary 1 is very difficult for all children and particularly so for the most vulnerable children who have additional support needs. Most schools now have a transition programme in place which is agreed by primary schools and their local secondary school. Such a programme involves planned visits of both staff and pupils to the receiving secondary school and often also involves visits to the feeder primary schools by staff from the secondary school.

When dealing with children with additional support needs, it is very important that receiving teachers fully understand the individual needs and barriers to learning so that planning for pupils can be done in advance of transfer. Onus is on the primary school to pass on all important information to the secondary school and on the latter to ensure that this information is communicated to all subject staff who will teach the pupil.

SUMMARY

Class teachers in the primary school have responsibility for the learning of all pupils in their class even when pupils have the additional support provided by a support for learning teacher. Assessment should be viewed as an integral part of teaching, and identification of needs is not a one-off process but should be part of a continuous process. Some pupils who have additional support needs will require individualised planning to meet their needs. The implementation of an IEP should take place as far as possible within a shared learning context. Such a plan is not designed for a pupil to work in isolation. Support for learning teachers should work collaboratively in classrooms. In addition to the five key areas of the primary curriculum, every class teacher is also concerned with educating the whole child. Self-esteem is often an issue affecting pupils who fail in the learning process, so personal and social development must always be as much of a consideration as curriculum aspects when planning a broad and balanced curriculum for all.

Partnership with parents and other professionals is essential when planning responses to pupil needs. Primary schools must identify their extended network of support, and lines of communication with the full range of professionals must be established. The transition stage is often when pupils with additional support needs are at their most vulnerable. Primary and secondary schools must work together to plan appropriately for this stage so that pupils feel supported in the process.

POINTS FOR REFLECTION

1 Do class teachers accept responsibility for the learning of all pupils in their class? To what extent does the view still prevail that it is the responsibility of other professionals to provide support exclusively for learners with additional needs?

2 To what extent have schools identified their extended network of support, and have the lines of communication been clearly defined for staff?

3 How would you know that all professionals in a primary school subscribe to the view that the education of the whole child is paramount? Is such a school likely to be more or less inclusive?

7 Additional support needs: secondary school

When a teacher calls a boy by his entire name it means trouble.

Mark Twain

For the past 40 years the comprehensive ideal has underpinned secondary education in Scotland. In the 1960s the emerging comprehensive schools had to face the challenge of catering for a wider range of young people with varying levels of ability. To a large extent this involved transforming our system of secondary schooling, which had traditionally been based firmly within a process of selection. Young people were allocated to schools according to their academic ability and the whole process was fuelled by selection. It would, however, be fair to say that some schools internalised the comprehensive ideal more readily than others. The keynote was change and this process involved rethinking the system of selection, the content and delivery of the curriculum, forms of organisation, methodology, teaching styles and provision of appropriate learning opportunities. In short the whole fabric of the traditional secondary school had to be re-examined. It is not difficult therefore to see the parallels between making comprehensive education a reality and the current emphasis upon developing inclusive education. The changes required in moving towards inclusion are not only of a similar scale to the move towards comprehensive schooling but they are also similar in nature.

Much of what has been said in the previous two chapters in relation to pre-5 education and primary education applies also to the secondary sector, and the overall aim is to extend the good practice already established into the secondary school. At the same time, however, it must be recognised that young people are becoming young adults, and as they enter the secondary school their needs may vary accordingly. This of course applies to all young people entering what for them is a new and exciting environment but for those with additional support needs the move to secondary can be a time when they feel particularly anxious and often a bit vulnerable. If the needs of this group of young people are to continue to be effectively met within the secondary school then systems must be in place which ensure:

- the young person's experience at the transition stage is coherent, continuous and progressive
- the curriculum on offer continues to be appropriate, accessible and inclusive
- effective support is available for all young people but particularly those with additional support needs
- effective identification and assessment procedures are in place
- high priority is given to working collaboratively
- learning and teaching is of a high quality, flexible and responsive to individual need.

Primary–secondary transition

It is vital that the channels of communication between the primary and secondary sectors are set up in a way which enables the exchange of information about the nature and range of the young person's difficulties and the additional support which must be in place before transfer.

In 1986 the 10–14 Report recommended a range of strategies aimed at improving the transition process. Although these recommendations were not officially accepted as national policy some of them were quickly internalised into the practice of the more forward-looking primary and secondary schools. These include:

- familiarisation visits to the secondary school by primary 7 pupils
- the creation of P7/S1 intersector curriculum projects linking the process of learning and teaching in P7 to that in S1
- visits throughout the P7 stage by guidance teachers, support for learning teachers and other teachers to plan the transition process, share information and teach
- the creation of more user-friendly literature about the secondary school and visits to these schools by parents before transition when their questions could be answered

- improved documentation exchanged between sectors, providing a balanced pupil profile indicating strengths and providing information which would assist in the anticipation of potential difficulties.

These are now fairly standard procedures in most primary and secondary schools and operate to ensure that the move from primary to secondary school is smooth and unproblematic for most young people, including those with additional support needs.

Boyd and Simpson (2003) support this view when they say that the 5–14 programme has had a positive impact on ensuring curricular continuity at the transition stage and that continuity in pastoral care and pupil support has also improved. However, they also make it clear that pedagogical continuity between sectors is still an issue which has not yet been resolved. Pedagogy in the primary school tends to be child-centred but to a large extent the secondary sector is still dominated by subject-centred pedagogy. This is an issue which is of concern for all young people but particularly those with additional support needs. Such a pedagogy tends to be less tolerant of individuals who do not fit into existing systems and is less likely to respond appropriately to diversity. It is not enough to simply pass on to the secondary school relevant information about young people when they enter primary 7. There must be evidence that this information results in appropriate action and is translated into practice through a pedagogy which recognises diversity and is capable of responding to individual need; this pedagogy still appears to be more evident in the primary sector.

Hamill and Boyd (2001) undertook a research study in one Scottish local authority which did not have any segregated schools and was attempting to set up in mainstream primary and secondary schools support systems aimed at including all young people with additional support needs. The research focused in particular upon the needs of those young people deemed by the authority to have more complex learning difficulties and who would traditionally have been placed in a segregated special school. Several important messages emerged from the research, which had an impact upon the P7 – S1 transition process and which need to be considered very carefully by education authorities who intend to go for full inclusion of all young people.

The majority of secondary school teachers involved in the research study (Hamill and Boyd 2001) did not appear to have fully internalised an understanding of what was meant by the term 'additional support needs'. They consistently referred to young people with mild or moderate difficulties as having severe or complex difficulties, and there was ample evidence to suggest that many teachers did not see young people who presented disruptive behaviour as having additional support needs.

There were, of course, also some primary school teachers who still took a view closely linked to the deficit model when talking about young people with additional support needs, but the majority of teachers in the primary sector appeared to have a clearer understanding of this term and were more aware of the nature and range of difficulties that these young people experienced. Thus the concept of additional support needs was not always shared by professionals across sectors, and many secondary school teachers in particular still did not appear to have internalised a clear understanding of the diversity of learners who had additional support needs.

Hamill and Boyd (2001) raised three particular areas of concern in relation to young people with additional support needs at the transition stage.

- Primary schools tended to be more receptive than secondary schools to a wide range of pupil needs and appeared to be more willing to adapt and cater for diversity. There was evidence to suggest that inclusion for some young people with additional support needs was only a viable prospect at the primary school stage.
- A number of parents expressed concern in relation to the continuity of support that their child received. They tended to speak highly of these experiences at the primary school stage but they often expressed serious reservations about the secondary school's ability to replicate this good practice. It must also be said that these parents had been given little or no opportunity to actually experience at first hand what additional support would be available in the secondary school and so their negative perceptions tended to be reinforced and confirmed.
- The senior managers and support for learning teachers in several secondary schools tended to feel that it was acceptable to think about the additional needs of young people only at the transition stage when they entered primary 7. This was particularly problematic in relation to those learners whose

needs were more complex and who depended on a coherent, long-term, cross-sectoral co-ordinated system of support if their needs were to be effectively addressed. More effective long-term planning was vital if the secondary schools were to be in a position to offer these young people the support required. This was an issue for both sectors and it was clear that in addition to concerns relating to the secondary sector there were some support teachers in primary schools who had not given enough thought to long-term planning in relation to the future needs of their pupils.

It would appear that schools are striving to ensure that the transition process is smooth for the majority of young people and there is evidence that the systems currently in place are generally sound However, in the case of young people whose additional support needs are perceived to be more complex, the transition process may be more problematic, and barriers to effective transition emerge which may not be easily resolved. There is a need to ensure that:

- all teachers share an understanding of additional support needs as a diverse, wide-ranging concept
- the views of parents whose children have additional support needs should be acknowledged as valid and taken into account, and opportunities should be available well in advance of the transition stage at P7 for them to visit the secondary school
- a long-term view is taken in relation to the additional support needs of some young people to ensure effective continuity and progression.

Providing an appropriate curriculum

At the secondary stage the continuum of additional support needs is still a priority and the nature and range of difficulties which give rise to these needs are in most respects similar to those experienced in the primary school. The principles underpinning good practice are fundamentally the same regardless of the educational context. However, at the secondary stage there are also differences which must be considered and these relate to the increasing demands made on young people in terms of:

- physical and emotional development
- the more complex organisation of the secondary school
- expectations of greater independence
- an expanded curriculum
- the vocational dimension
- preparation for the transition to adulthood.

The above list is presented on page 49 of the SOED (1994a) report on 'Effective Provision for Special Educational Needs', which makes it clear that in the secondary sector the needs of young people can change fairly rapidly. Thus secondary schools need to be capable of responding flexibly and making the necessary adjustments required to meet need.

The curriculum is central to the whole process of meeting need and responding to diversity. 'A Manual of Good Practice in Special Educational Needs' (SOEID 1998) outlines the basic principles in relation to the curriculum, which apply equally to all young people. The curriculum must satisfy the principles of breadth, balance, progression, continuity and coherence, and all young people must have an equal entitlement to a curriculum in line with national guidance, i.e. 5–14, Standard Grade and Higher Still. Equal opportunities must be provided for all to achieve excellence, to be set high expectations and to have their achievements valued in an inclusive environment. Meeting these requirements may present challenges to secondary schools. It must be remembered, however, that the school has a responsibility to ensure the above principles are translated into practice for all young people. To do so effectively, schools must carefully consider how to implement the process of differentiation and the role of individual educational programmes within this overarching process.

Individualised educational programmes (IEPs)

One of the major challenges which has faced secondary schools since the early 1980s, and continues to do so, is differentiation. This key strategy underpins effective teaching and learning and is the vehicle through which additional support needs will be met. Individualised educational plans provide the foundation upon which effective differentiation can be planned and implemented, and all young people in the secondary school with additional support needs should have an IEP.

When young people with additional support needs enter the secondary school they will bring with them from primary school an IEP which will provide valuable information that can be used to ensure continuity and progression in relation to learning and support. The secondary school must ensure that this process of individualised educational planning continues throughout the young person's secondary school career as it will provide the written plan outlining the steps to be taken to enable the young person to achieve agreed goals. 'A Manual of Good Practice in Special Educational Needs' provides excellent guidance in relation to IEPs.

Basically the IEP acts as a planning framework for teachers who use it to ensure the curriculum on offer, and the teaching and learning experiences available, are appropriate. The IEP can vary in nature and scale, and the content will be dictated by the needs of the young person. Table 7.1 adapted from the Manual of Good Practice, provides a summary of the points which need to be addressed by the school in planning an implementing an individual education plan.

Table 7.1 An individualised educational programme should ...

be strongly rooted within the process of careful individual assessment which will inform target setting
contain a set of SMART Targets (Specific, Measurable, Achievable, Relevant, and Timed) to be achieved by the learner as he/she moves towards the long-term target
ensure the young person has the opportunity to contribute towards the process agreeing the targets, evaluating success and planning next steps
be used by staff to plan progression and monitor the effectiveness of teaching and learning
include a series of short- and long-term targets which should be agreed, but a particular IEP will focus upon a few specific targets and more advanced targets will feature in subsequent IEPs
include long-term targets generally covering a whole school session. These should be broken down into short-term targets achievable over a 6–8 week period. For some learners it will be necessary to further break down these targets into specific objectives or extend long-term targets to indicate what might be achieved over a one or two year period
identify success criteria which will indicate when a target has been achieved
where possible ensure parents are involved in drawing up the IEP; they should have access to the IEP and have a say in how it is implemented, monitored and reviewed
outline the level of support to be provided, identify the staff involved, record the nature, duration and frequency of their input, and indicate resources required

Effective differentiation is based upon a system of IEPs which takes full account of the factors outlined in Table 7.1. Differentiation is therefore the key implementation strategy which ensures what is written in the IEP becomes a reality.

Differentiation

The aim of differentiation is to maximise opportunity for learners and aid access to an appropriate curriculum. It is important to re-emphasise the point made in Chapter 3 that differentiation is a process which should apply to all learners and is not something that relates exclusively to those young people who have additional support needs. However, for those learners with additional support needs, differentiation is vital to ensuring that teaching and learning opportunities match the IEP targets.

It is very important to see differentiation as a process that can be widely applied within the classroom. Too often it is viewed purely in terms of resources; it is quite common to hear teachers talk about differentiation in this narrow sense of differentiating worksheets at three levels: extension, core and remediation. This is important but it is only a very small part of what differentiation is all about.

Differentiation, as outlined earlier in this book, is fundamentally about catering for diversity. There is no doubt that if it is to be put into practice it will present challenges to teachers in many secondary schools. It is important to emphasise the point that there are teachers in all secondary schools who have risen to the challenge of differentiation and are striving to ensure they are effectively meeting the needs of all learners. At the same time there are also teachers who still prefer not to take on the challenge of differentiation and do not see it as a vital prerequisite to effective teaching and learning. Moving thinking forward can be very slow and we must accept that we have not yet won the hearts and minds of all teachers as far as differentiation is concerned. However, in those schools where the principle of differentiation is strongly rooted, teachers are well aware of the range of areas to which the differentiation process can be applied. These are summarised in Figure 7.1.

Figure 7.1 Differentiation

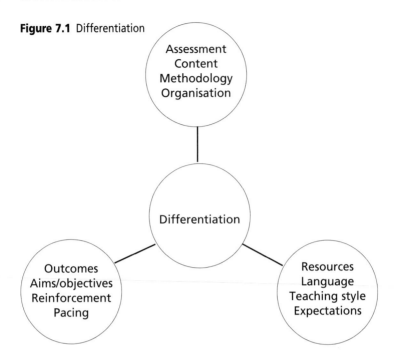

The SOED (1994b) report 'Special Needs Within the 5–14 Curriculum – Support for Learning' sums up the process of differentiation as applying to all effective teaching but it is particularly important in meeting the challenge of ensuring that those with additional support needs access the curriculum. However, as one would expect, the teacher is as always the key and he/she must be prepared to adopt a curricular model as opposed to the traditional deficit model when thinking about the reasons why some young people have difficulty with learning. This is central to the teacher's understanding and implementation of differentiation. All teachers must ask themselves the crucial question: which of the two models as outlined in Figure 7.2 and Figure 7.3, best describes my professional view?

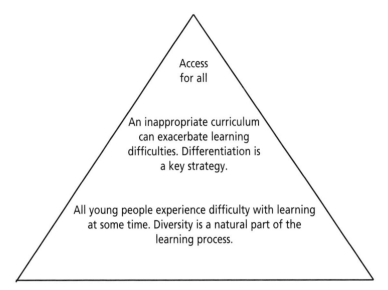

Figure 7.2 The curriculum model

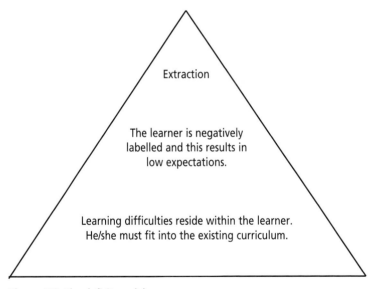

Figure 7.3 The deficit model

The model adopted will indicate clearly the educational philosophy underpinning the teacher's perceptions of his/her role in meeting the additional support needs of learners who experience difficulty in learning. It will determine the extent to which the teacher accepts one of the basic principles outlined in 1978 by HMI in their report on young people with learning difficulties in Scottish schools when they said that all learners in the school, including those with learning difficulty, were ultimately the responsibility of the class teacher albeit with support provided by support for learning teachers and other professionals.

The deficit model encourages the belief that schools are there to adapt learners to what is perceived as normal, whereas the curriculum model emphasises mutual respect and the need for schools to celebrate and cater for differing talents. In essence, therefore, effective teachers differentiate because they know it is at the heart of the teaching/learning process.

Susskind (1989) provides food for thought when he suggests that schools which do not make every effort to cater for diversity through differentiation tend to promote mediocrity and conformity among learners.

The checklist in Table 7.2 should be of use to teachers who wish to undertake a differentiation audit. It is aimed at encouraging professionals to think about their classroom practice. Teachers should tick box 1 if they use the strategy frequently, box 2 if the strategy is used occasionally and box 3 if the strategy is seldom or never used.

Table 7.2 Differentiation checklist

	1	2	3
I pay careful attention to the design and layout of all resources I use.			
I encourage pupils to work individually, in pairs and in groups.			
I set pupils different tasks according to their ability.			
I vary my teaching style and methodology to suit the needs of pupils.			
I organise my teaching to suit the varying pace/rate of learning of pupils.			
I recognise and am sensitive to the diverse needs of all learners.			
I make appropriate use of ICT in my teaching.			
I have well organised and managed retrieval and storage systems.			
I cater for choice by providing a range of relevant tasks.			
I accept that the teaching of study skills is part of my job.			
I try to motivate pupils by matching tasks to their interests.			
I do not always expect the same outcome (product) from all pupils.			
I provide opportunities for pupils to record their work in different ways.			
I make full use of a wide range of assessment activities.			
I do not assume previous knowledge but alert pupils in advance in relation to revision/preparation that may be necessary.			
I give pupils different types of feedback and reinforcement.			
I build in different learning routes for different pupils.			
I provide individual support when needed.			
I work co-operatively with colleagues to enhance learning in my classroom.			
I make the assessment criteria explicit to all pupils.			
I use individual education plans (IEPs) for pupils who need them.			
I make course aims/objectives explicit to all pupils.			
I encourage pupils to express their views and opinions.			
I evaluate my teaching and adapt it accordingly.			

Support for learning

In discussing the organisation of secondary schools, Lennon (2003, p. 426) says 'that the child deficit model criticised by Warnock over twenty years ago has been reinforced by generations of teachers and remains part of the general consciousness of almost everyone who works in Scottish education'. He goes on to say that this model still dominates the thinking of many secondary school teachers and is a powerful determinant of their professional attitude. It would appear that, in many secondary schools, learners with additional support needs continue to be seen as a barrier to the effective teaching of the subject and as an obstacle to the effective learning of their peers. Despite all of the rhetoric in relation to inclusion, in reality in some schools it would appear that little has changed for these young people.

In their studies on inclusive education, Hamill and Boyd (2001, 2002) shadowed young people with additional support needs in 25 secondary schools and found that increasing numbers of schools were moving away from mixed-ability teaching and using a system of streaming where young people were assigned to classes for a given subject depending on their attainment in that subject. Several teachers in these schools referred to the bottom, middle and top sets when discussing attainment and the vast majority of individuals shadowed in these schools were in the so-called bottom sets. The researchers found that the composition of these sets varied very little from subject to subject and that in fact these bottom sets closely resembled the traditional remedial classes.

Of course this is not the intended purpose of streaming; nonetheless this was the reality for the young people with additional support needs in these schools. This raises a crucial question about the compatibility of the drive to raise attainment and the move towards full mainstream inclusion. Thus as we move forward in supporting young people with additional support needs within inclusive schools we must always remember that, although the principle we are striving for is accepted by most secondary teachers, there are still barriers to be broken down. Overcoming these will require a fundamental rethinking of how we should organise learning in ways that ensure all learners benefit. As already mentioned, inclusion is about transforming schools not about fitting learners into existing systems.

Having sounded this cautionary note it is important to make it clear that most schools continue to try to find ways of ensuring they have in place effective provision for young people with additional support needs. All schools now have support for learning teachers who fulfil a range of roles. These include:

- supporting on a one-to-one or small-group basis young people with more complex needs, or providing short term support in particular circumstances
- working co-operatively in class with subject colleagues supporting them and the young people
- acting as a cross-curricular consultant advising on appropriate curriculum and differentiation
- providing relevant in-house CPD opportunities for colleagues in the area of additional support needs.

Education authorities in Scotland are keen to ensure that their support for learning teachers undertake an appropriate programme of study. Most universities have provided postgraduate programmes in support for learning since the early 1990s, and the majority of support for learning teachers have already gained this qualification or will in future take up the opportunity to do so.

In recent years attention in secondary schools has focused on the development of more holistic approaches to meeting the needs of young people with additional support needs. These approaches are summarised in 'A Manual of Good Practice in Special Educational Needs' (SOEID 1998, p.63):

- The school policy makes it clear that all staff have a responsibility to support young people with additional support needs.
- Specialist staff are involved in helping young people assess their own learning and agree learning targets.
- Specialist staff provide support to class teachers through co-operative teaching, professional development, working individually with young people and sharing their expertise through consultancy.
- The school should pay due regard without discrimination to the disabilities, gender, religious persuasion, racial origins and cultural and linguistic background of all young people and parents.

- Policies and procedures are in place for ensuring effective liaison with specialist support services, and a responsibility and co-ordinating role is allocated to a member of staff.
- Additional support is provided for young people over transition periods and procedures are in place to evaluate and review the transition process.
- Appropriate technology, including information and communication technology is provided to help learners access the curriculum.
- The school policy acknowledges the key role of parents and the importance of developing partnership at the earliest stage.
- Procedures are in place for securing adequate and appropriate resources to ensure schools are able to meet their responsibilities in relation to supporting young people with additional support needs.
- The school development plan includes arrangements to provide continuing professional development opportunities for staff to extend their understanding and awareness in relation to additional support needs.
- The CPD needs of specialist support staff are addressed to ensure they stay abreast of current developments and new technologies.

The above provides an excellent framework for secondary schools to review and audit the nature, range and quality of support. However, it is not only support for learning teachers who have a specific role in relation to those young people who have additional support needs. Support is also provided by guidance teachers, behaviour support teachers and other professionals such as speech and language therapists, social workers and educational psychologists who form an extended support team. Many schools are now looking at how the work of all of these specialist staff can be integrated within one overall support services network. This move towards a more holistic approach to meeting additional support needs has been influenced by two important reports both published by SEED.

The first of these appeared in 1999 and was entitled 'New Community Schools: The Prospectus'. It introduced the new community school initiative aimed at promoting social inclusion, destroying the cycle of underachievement and ensuring every young person maximised his/her full potential. The report acknowledged that this would require radically new integrated approaches to enable appropriate action to be taken to meet the needs of vulnerable young people. Following on from this initiative in 2001 the 'Better Behaviour – Better Learning' report, which examined issues of indiscipline, presented a strong case for bringing all professionals involved in supporting young people together as one integrated team. It was recommended that 'schools should give consideration to integrating the work of learning support, behaviour support and guidance into a single overall framework of pupil support in order to achieve a more holistic approach to supporting the needs of all young people' (SEED 2001, p. 14). The need for a holistic, professionally integrated approach is best summed up by considering a profile of a (ficticious) learner with additional support needs.

KYLIE: A MINI PROFILE

Kylie is in P7 and enters S1 shortly. She has difficulty in learning in all areas of literacy/numeracy and stutters badly under stress. She has received good support in primary but she is still at level B (5–14) in language/mathematics. She enjoys music and PE and has shown some ability as an artist. She does not appear to have any school friends and she is becoming isolated, showing some reluctance to talk to either her teacher or her peers. Kylie's attendance has begun to deteriorate, she seems very anxious about going to what she calls the 'big school' and her teacher is concerned as when Kylie does speak she says she is useless at everything. Her self-esteem is very low and, to make matters worse, she is now beginning to present some challenging behaviour and is becoming sullen and moody. She got into a fight with another girl who called her a 'dummy' and both where excluded from school. At the last parent's night her mum said she was worried about Kylie and there were problems at home involving social services and the police. She has been referred to a psychologist, and placement in a special school is being considered. Kylie's mum attended a special school and she is adamant this will not happen to Kylie who is now even more anxious and stressed.

If Kylie's additional support needs are to be met the integrated support team must consider the following questions:

1 What exactly are the young person's needs?
2 Who is responsible for identifying the nature of her difficulties and how will this be done?

3 Who will be responsible for ensuring an integrated support plan will be put in place which addresses these needs holistically?

4 Who will provide the additional support and where and when will it be provided?

5 How will all relevant professionals be made aware of their roles/responsibilities and those of their colleagues within the integrated support team?

6 How will the integrated support plan be communicated to other relevant staff and how will it link into the IEP?

7 How will the whole process be monitored and evaluated?

The concept of an integrated support service is still not the norm in many secondary schools as it will require a rethinking of traditional practice. In some situations it will involve a fairly radical transformation of the professional culture of a school and as always such change is likely to prove to be challenging, especially where attitudes are entrenched. Difficulties are more likely to emerge in situations where the professionals feel their role and expertise is being threatened as opposed to understanding that this approach does not mean a dilution of their specialist role but will involve finding ways of making these specialist roles complementary and child-centred.

Behaviour an issue for inclusion

The 'Count Us In' report (2003), which examined the issue of inclusion in Scottish schools, identified one group of young people with additional support needs who presented particularly difficult challenges to schools. These young people experience social, emotional and behavioural difficulties and as a result they are often alienated, marginalised and excluded. Hamill and Boyd (2000, 2001, and 2002) found that this was a major issue for most secondary school teachers in particular, who tended to identify inclusion with this group of young people whose behaviour could be challenging. In common with other studies (Cooper 1993; O'Brien 1998; Porter 2000) Hamill and Boyd concluded that when the concept of inclusion focuses upon young people whose behaviour can be disruptive the issues become highly charged and emotive.

The majority of teachers when asked if this group of young people had special educational needs (additional support needs) made it very clear that in their opinion these young people made a conscious choice to be disruptive and as a result they forfeited the right to mainstream education. These young people were consistently described as 'bad pupils' who manipulated the system, and by continuing to include them the system was in fact rewarding their bad behaviour. These young people were seen to pose the biggest barrier to inclusion within secondary schools, and teachers' experiences of working with this group tended to colour their overall view of inclusion. In general most teachers were reasonably happy to make an effort to include young people with sensory, physical and less complex learning difficulties but this positive outlook was stretched to the limit when the young person's behaviour was disruptive and there was evidence that this could result in teachers rejecting the whole inclusive process.

The report of the national discipline task group ('Better Behaviour – Better Learning', SEED 2001) supported the growth in provision of flexible support for young people with social, emotional and behavioural difficulties, including setting up in-house support bases outwith the normal classroom environment in secondary schools. Hamill and Boyd studied several of these support bases and found evidence that they did to some extent offer an alternative to exclusion. On the other hand, many teachers said they did not feel any real ownership of these new initiatives, imposed on them by government, local authorities and educationalists who don't have to face the challenges that inclusion brings. They saw this as evidence that their views on inclusion were not valued and were often dismissed out of hand if they did not conform to the received wisdom of those who knew best. Teachers do not automatically oppose inclusion; in general they too want it to work in practice. Thus the voice of the teacher who has to make inclusion a reality must be heard. In inclusive schools, teachers should themselves feel included and that their views are welcomed. In such schools potential barriers to inclusion are openly discussed and ways to overcome them are identified and implemented in a sense of partnership where the teacher is seen to be the key player in facilitating essential changes to the positive supportive culture which characterises the inclusive school.

SUMMARY

Transition from primary to secondary school is an important process for all young people. For those with additional support needs, continuity of support is crucial and this requires careful planning and preparation. Good practice in most secondary schools has evolved over the past decade or so. However, subject-centred pedagogy still dominates and this can result in an inappropriate curriculum which does not meet the needs of all learners.

Differentiation is often equated with meeting the needs of those who require additional support and, although this is very important, it must be seen as a strategy which is relevant to all learners.

Most secondary schools have Support for Learning Departments staffed by specialist teachers. These teachers work collaboratively with their subject colleagues to provide additional support for young people who experience difficulty in learning. Most schools are now considering how they can bring all support professionals (e.g. support for learning, behaviour and guidance specialists) together to form one overall support service. Many teachers now believe that disruptive behaviour is presenting particular challenges and that this is having an adverse effect on the whole inclusion initiative.

POINTS FOR REFLECTION

1. How would you know that a secondary school and its associated primaries had in place a transition process which took into account the needs of all learners, and in particular those with additional support needs?

2. Is there a clear understanding among professionals what an IEP is, what it should contain and how it should be used to support young people?

3. In secondary schools is differentiation seen as a vital strategy which is relevant to the needs of all learners and is there evidence that teachers use it to cater for diversity?

8 Redefining the role of the special school

> The mediocre teacher tells. The good teacher explains. The superior teacher demonstrates. The great teacher inspires.
>
> **William Arthur Ward**

Presumption of mainstreaming

In Chapter 1 we discussed briefly the role of special schools within the context of inclusion. All of the current legislation in relation to additional support needs makes it clear that, notwithstanding the commitment to mainstream inclusion, there will continue to be a need for some diversity in provision. It is now acknowledged that there will still be a need for some special schools providing integrated support systems and incorporating the health, education and care needs of young people whose needs are significant and/or complex. However, it must be recognised that there is now in law a presumption that mainstream will always in the first instance be considered as the most appropriate learning environment for all young people; this is already making an impact on the nature and range of our present system of special schooling, and will continue to do so.

Although there does not appear to be an immediate prospect of closures of special schools, it is inevitable that ultimately some special schools will close, and those that remain will need to redefine their role in order to provide appropriate support for the young people with additional support needs who will continue to need their specialist services. Special schools will need to work in partnership with mainstream schools and the wider inter-agency support services to provide mutual support systems. These schools will be expected to evolve as centres of excellence, capitalising on and developing further their strengths. They will no longer be seen as places where young people spend their entire school careers and they will play a significant role as part of an evolving integral system of inclusive education. It is likely that as we progress through the twenty-first century there will be fewer special schools and those which remain will focus on those young people who experience the most complex/ multiple difficulties. We do, however, have to understand that one size can never fit the diverse range of individual need which exists. Effectively responding to the diversity of need implies diversity of provision. Although our ultimate goal will be mainstream provision, we must accept that inclusion does not automatically equate with mainstreaming, nor does it necessarily signal the end for all special schools. We must be pragmatic and see that inclusion is fundamentally about ensuring young people are educated in the environment which best suits their needs, and this could be mainstream or special school.

Moving to mainstream

Currently in Scotland there still exists a range of specialist provision. There are schools operating outwith mainstream provision which provide support for discrete groups of learners with specific needs. Some other special schools are more generic and cater for a wider range of needs, and some young people are educated in special units attached to mainstream schools. In 2004 Audit Scotland, in partnership with HMI, examined the current pattern of additional support needs provision across Scotland. The following key points emerge from their report 'Moving to Mainstream' (p. 18).

- There are currently 44,000 young people identified as having additional support needs educated in publicly funded schools This is 5.9% of the school population.
- Around 8,200 young people with additional support needs (19%) are educated in publicly funded special schools and the percentage of young people in special schools has remained steady for the past seven years.
- The majority of young people with additional support needs are currently in mainstream schools but 3% of these spend all of their time in special units attached to mainstream schools.
- 13% of young people with additional support needs in mainstream schools spend their time partly in mainstream classes and partly in special units.

The audit report concludes that as a result of the presumption of mainstreaming the numbers currently educated in special schools will continue to decrease and the biggest impact will be upon those young people currently labelled as having moderate learning difficulties (MLD) and those with physical or sensory impairments. This report also reinforces the view that some special schools will continue to operate but they will serve the needs of a much smaller group of young people with complex and multiple needs.

The challenge for special schools

It is clear therefore that the educational context in which special schools have operated is changing rapidly. Inclusion is here to stay, and all professionals are being encouraged to internalise an inclusive philosophy. The majority of professionals have now taken on board the view that the principles underpinning inclusive education are sound and we must all now play our part in making inclusion a reality in practice. The part to be played by those in special schools will be particularly significant. The starting point should be the realisation that we must proceed with caution and be careful that we do not throw the baby out with the bath water. To avoid this situation we must recognise the excellent work which has been done in special schools and which we now hope to harness in making our mainstream schools more inclusive.

Many special schools have provided a rich, stimulating learning environment where young people have been given the opportunity to develop to their full potential. These schools have traditionally been characterised as having a positive ethos and staff who understand the needs of the young people they support. It should be acknowledged that for some teachers this is still a persuasive argument for maintaining segregated special schools. The aim is to find ways of building upon the strengths of the special school sector, and care must be taken to ensure that these positive features are incorporated into emerging provision. If, however, we are truly going to move forward in relation to inclusion it is important to think about and address the arguments often put forward to support segregated schooling.

Farrell (1996) points out that segregated provision is likely to be more cost-effective and there is evidence in the report

'Moving to Mainstream' to support the view 'the inclusion of pupils (ASN) is likely to increase costs' (Audit Scotland 2003, p. 57). Farrell goes on to suggest that in special schools young people benefit from a curriculum suited to their needs and that the degree of individual planning involved in meeting need is not feasible within the mainstream school. The case for special schools also focuses on the view that parental support may be more forthcoming in segregated schools; teachers who teach in these schools choose to do so and are likely to be highly motivated; and vulnerable children are safer in these environments. As already mentioned, some professionals still adhere to the view that segregated schooling provides the most effective learning climate for young people with additional support needs and we must be careful in our pursuit of mainstreaming not to simply ignore these arguments. These views should be recognised as valid and every effort must be made to take account of them within the inclusion debate.

However, the inclusion agenda continues to drive home the message that although special schools have played an important role their existence was based on what is now recognised as a fundamentally flawed philosophy. Segregated provision was based on a medical model which focused upon perceived deficits in the child. Hall (1996) argues that it will not be easy to challenge thinking which has become internalised over a long period of time. But this thinking must be challenged if we are to move forward and this will require a change of hearts and minds and a willingness to accept the strong arguments against segregated schooling, which have been around for a fairly long time.

In 1982, for example, Tomlinson was one of the first to suggest that segregated schooling was in fact a form of social control, designed more to help mainstream schools function more effectively than to meet individual needs. Several other writers took this argument still further, presenting evidence that although special schools were set up for the good of those taught within them the underlying message they sent out was that the learners were less valued, negatively labelled and socially isolated. (Dyson 1997). Corbett (2001) adds considerably to this debate about segregated schooling when she takes a strong stance against exclusionist practice but at the same time makes it clear that in her opinion mainstream schools have much to learn from the special education sector. She cautions against the dangers inherent when so-called inclusion purists respond negatively to the special education sector. Therefore, if real change is to occur, those who currently work in the segregated sector must take on and address the challenges inherent in the move towards mainstream inclusion.

Redefining the role of the special school

As we have seen, it is inevitable that the impact of inclusion will result in the fact that a number of our special schools will close, and those that remain will need to think through and redefine their role. We must start by building upon existing good practice and demonstrate how this practice can support inclusion. Special schools have over the years developed a wide range of knowledge, skills and experience in relation to caring for and supporting young people with additional support needs. In future these schools will increasingly work in partnership with the mainstream school as part of an inclusive education system. Together they must find the key to unlock the potential within our special schools and harness it so that it can be shared and utilised to benefit all learners regardless of the context in which they are taught. As far back as 1978 Warnock emphasised that there was a considerable amount of valuable expertise within the segregated sector which could be more widely shared and more effectively utilised. The idea of the special school as a resource centre emerged but this idea has been slow to evolve in Scotland. This theme has been taken up in the report 'Moving Forward! Additional Support Needs' (SEED 2003) which emphasises that mainstream and special schools can learn from each other and that exchange of knowledge and experience can be facilitated between both sectors.

Cheminais (2003) suggests that special schools should consider compiling a menu indicating the range of services they might offer to their mainstream partners. She outlines some examples taken from the DFES report 'Inclusive Schooling: Children with Special Educational Needs' (2001) of how special schools might develop as centres of excellence sharing their resources with mainstream. These are:

- providing an outreach programme to mainstream schools aimed at supporting young people with additional support needs
- providing continuing professional opportunities to teachers and other staff in mainstream schools

- working together to ensure the effective identification and assessment of need
- working co-operatively, providing support and giving advice to colleagues in mainstream schools
- sharing resources and exchanging aspects of good practice with mainstream schools
- producing relevant teaching resources and other materials to support colleagues and young people in mainstream schools
- enhancing networking by creating inter-school forums and inclusion teams
- planning joint initiatives, social events and projects in partnership
- establishing web pages linked to other national websites aimed at promoting and sharing good inclusive practice.

Although the idea of the special school as a resource centre or centre of excellence is now fairly well established across Scotland, there is still a lot of work to be done to make it an accepted reality. Nonetheless a number of special schools are at the forefront of these developments and have taken the initiative. This is acknowledged in 'Moving Forward! Additional Support for Learning' (SEED 2003) where it is highlighted that specialist provision can play a vital role in preparing young people to attend mainstream schools. Priority is given to a two-way exchange of knowledge, skills and experience. The report gives two examples of good practice in this area.

1 Mainstream and special schools working together to develop an elaborated curriculum for young people with more complex learning needs
2 A school for blind pupils producing curricular materials in braille to help support young people with visual impairment in mainstream schools

It is now becoming clear that special schools in the twenty-first century will need to be prepared to take on this multi-purpose role. It should, however, be kept in mind that this is not a new vision for special schools. It has been taking shape since the early 1990s and is now firmly established in principle and increasingly evident in good practice. Hegarty (1994) advocated a new type of specialist institution which extended our thinking well beyond the traditional view of the special school. His ideas are still valid and provide insight into what such a multi-dimensional school might look like. Young people supported in these schools will have more complex and/or multiple needs and although they will be supported in these new specialist centres they will also have the opportunity to join their peers and share in the mainstream experience. Hegarty presents a framework outlining some of the functions these new special schools will fulfil. They will:

- be a source of information on all matters relating to special educational needs
- conduct assessments
- provide advice, consultancy and support
- engage in curriculum and material development
- evaluate software, equipment and other resources
- conduct research and undertake experimental projects
- contribute to professional development
- be a resource for parents
- provide counselling and careers advice

Staff in these special schools will at all times be working in partnership with their colleagues in mainstream schools to ensure that additional support needs are effectively identified and met. The key will be the creation of an integrated support framework with the partners sharing experience, learning from each other and working together to resolve difficulties and solve problems imaginatively. As already indicated, the special school will play a significant role in these developments but we must be wary of implying in any way that they are the dominant partners. A true partnership is based on equality, particularly in the decision-making process which must be seen to be transparent, taking account of all viewpoints and fundamentally putting the young person's needs at the centre.

Inclusive partnerships – special schools and mainstream schools

Developing inclusive partnerships linking the special schools and mainstream schools will be a two-way process and one innovative way forward might be to think in terms of clusters. Evans and Lunt (1994) suggest that clusters provide a collaborative approach to meeting additional support needs and describe a cluster as 'a relatively stable and long term commitment among a group of schools to share resources and decision making about an area of school activity' (p. 92). The concept of the cluster is helpful in that it conveys a sense of partnership based on collaboration, negotiation and joint planning. Effective clusters will also include a range of agencies such as health, social work, and psychological services and they will provide a forum where all professionals can work together to identify and meet the additional support needs of young people holistically. Dyson and Gains (1993) also described what they perceived to be effective clustering arrangements. They emphasised the role of the special school as a resource base at the heart of the cluster providing a range of support services. These authors present several factors which they believe support the development of clusters:

- The competitive model for developing special needs, which has for many years dominated our thinking, is now accepted as outdated and inefficient.
- Local authorities will continue to allocate resources but are increasingly finding it difficult to sustain this level of resourcing given the pace of change particularly in relation to inclusion.
- As budgets are devolved to school level, senior managers will now be expected to take the lead in co-ordinating decisions about the use of resources in meeting additional support needs.

The local authorities will also need to rethink their strategy in the light of clustering. Their role will become one of enabler, ensuring that they have in place appropriate structures which promote an environment where clusters thrive. These structures will provide a supportive context within which special schools have the opportunity to clarify their wider service role and find the best way to market their new status. At the same time mainstream schools will capitalise on the enabling structure to think about their contribution to the cluster and to audit the skills and expertise they bring to the partnership.

Partnership can be a fragile concept and it can easily break down. If it is not to simply become another buzzword it must be set within a strong framework with sound principles understood and shared by all, regardless of the context in which they work. Some fundamental questions need to be addressed openly and honestly by all professionals entering into the inclusive partnership. Do all professionals:

- share the same inclusive philosophy and understand the concept of inclusion
- understand what the young people will gain from it
- recognise each other's skills/expertise
- share the same positive attitudes and expectations of learners
- value each other's contribution and listen to each other
- accept the importance of sharing teaching expertise and teaching facilities
- accept that they may have to work within unfamiliar contexts
- see the need to undertake joint staff development
- accept that change is inevitable
- appreciate each other's strengths and limitations
- internalise non-hierarchical styles of working based on collaborative practice
- accept that their role is first and foremost child-centred?

Earlier in this chapter we discussed the work of Hegarty (1994) and looked in particular at some of the roles which might be taken on by the special school within the context of the inclusion partnership. A considerable amount of research has shown what mainstream schools want from their special school partners. Fletcher-Campbell and Kington (2000) sum up these expectations by focusing on the mainstream perception of the high-quality specialist knowledge seen to reside within special schools and their aim to access this state-of-the-art specialist knowledge to benefit the young people with additional support needs educated in the mainstream context. Mainstream teachers are also keen to utilise the expertise of their special school colleagues to fill in perceived gaps in their own expertise and to provide hands-on practical help. It is clear what special schools have to offer mainstream colleagues but this partnership also involves the mainstream school and, as one would expect, the mainstream school has much to offer. The following list has been taken from Cheminais (2003). The mainstream school can offer the following to their special school partners:

- Access to specialist curriculum facilities and to a wider range of equipment, i.e. well-equipped science and language laboratories, up-to-date design and technology equipment, sports facilities, recording studios and extensive musical equipment. All of this helps to broaden curricular coverage and enables access to an enhanced range of learning experiences for young people with additional support needs.

- Access to a more extensive range of subject expertise and teaching in various areas of the curriculum, i.e. modern languages, music, ICT, physical education and art and design.
- More opportunity to ensure that the needs of learners are set within current curriculum guidelines as they apply to all learners, not just those with additional support needs.
- Greater experience of teambuilding and working in teams to develop policy.
- More experience in middle management, subject leadership and subject co-ordination.
- Positive peer role models for young people from special schools.
- Real-life experiences in the wider learning community environment helping to develop personal and social skills.
- More experience of marketing schools within the wider community context and greater experience of exploring and developing community links.

Thus both partners have much to offer and both must play their part in the central task of developing more inclusive educational cross-sector practice. This will involve redefining the role of the special school, transferring resources to mainstream, and the transformation of mainstream schools so that they fit the needs of all young people rather than trying to fit young people into existing systems. Inclusive schools will therefore be able to respond to a diverse range of needs and all learners within them will be part of one community where everyone has equality of opportunity.

Barriers to partnership

As one would expect, putting integrated inclusive systems in place will not be easy and it is likely that barriers will emerge which have the potential to inhibit the smooth path towards inclusive partnerships. It is important that we acknowledge and reflect on these potential barriers and take full account of them when planning the way forward. Teachers will naturally play a crucial role, and great care must be taken in how these new initiatives are presented to them. Currently in Scotland many teachers feel that they are being swamped by a plethora of new initiatives all demanding their time and attention. There is danger that inclusion is seen simply as part of this initiative overload and as such it will simply remain at the level of rhetoric; a good but unworkable idea. Adequate funding will also be needed if the concept of inclusive partnership is to become a reality. Creating a vision is one thing; translating it in to practice requires not only careful planning but also ensuring the finance is available to make it work.

Inspirational ideas often flounder because those who hold the purse strings are unable or unwilling to adequately finance them. Competing academic pressures on mainstream schools in particular present another potential barrier and it is easy to see that this can result in some confusion when schools have to find ways of resolving what are often perceived to be two irreconcilable pressures, i.e. raising attainment and implementing inclusive practice.

A further pressure facing many schools relates to the availability of staff. Schools are increasingly finding it difficult to recruit teachers who want to work in the field of additional support needs, and this also applies to vital para-professionals such as classroom assistants, particularly those who will take on roles specifically linked to supporting young people with additional support needs. This leads to another very important issue, that of appropriate continuing professional development which crucially underpins the success of inclusive partnerships. If this is not in place at the outset then it is difficult to see how progress will be made. Finally, barriers can result when school timetables lack flexibility, when schools are distant geographically and when administrative and organisational systems are rigid and incompatible.

Change is never easy and, as the process evolves and takes shape, barriers will emerge which have to be overcome. This is a natural part of the change process. If we are aware of what these barriers are likely to be, we will be in a better position to face and resolve the challenge they may pose in developing inclusive practice aimed at meeting the needs of young people with additional support needs. To move forward, it is important to think about and find ways of resolving areas of conflict or overcoming obstacles to progress. The clear message seems to be that inclusive partnerships are the way forward but we should proceed with caution. We must be realistic and responsible; this will involve:

- ensuring those who have to make inclusion work, particularly teachers, have a sense of ownership of the policy as opposed to having it imposed on them
- maintaining a continuum of services as opposed to simply internalising the view that full mainstream inclusion is the only feasible course of action
- encouraging schools to develop inclusive practice which is tailored to the needs of their community rather than taking a 'one model fits all' approach
- ensuring a realistic stance in relation to the human, physical and material resources which will be needed to make inclusion a reality
- setting up a system for evaluating and monitoring the effectiveness of provision and building in an ability to respond appropriately
- listening to the views of parents and young people and actively promoting discussion and the sharing of views
- considering staff needs as well as the needs of learners by ensuring ongoing professional development is available to all staff.

Experiencing segregation – pros and cons

One group whose voice is often missing from the debate on inclusion is those who have direct experience of segregated schooling. This seems surprising as it is logical that these are the people who can tell us about the reality of segregation. Professionals must provide opportunities for these voices to be heard, listen to them and take account of them. As one would expect, there is no simple answer; the picture is complex and covers a range of views. Nonetheless, all of the views expressed are valid and if the aim is to construct an inclusive system we must acknowledge the voices of experience.

Cook, Swain and French (2003) looked at inclusion from the point of view of one group of young people whose additional support needs resulted from their physical disabilities. The special school these young people had attended was closing and the majority were being transferred to mainstream schools as part of an inclusion initiative. These authors undertook a research project which focused on what they called 'voices from segregated schooling'. In essence young people were asked their views in relation to being excluded and what they thought about the move towards an inclusive education system. In general the young people were happy to rally under the flag of inclusion. They wanted to be educated alongside their able-bodied friends, to share common experiences and to be part of a wider, more diverse learning community. Inclusion was seen to have a powerful psychological dimension which prioritised a sense of belonging and removed the feeling of detachment from many of their peers.

At the same time, however, these young people made it clear that there were several positive aspects linked to their experiences of segregated schools. They emphasised that strong bonds had been established because they had been part of a community of individuals with similar needs. At the same time they highlighted the positive personal and social benefits of having the opportunity to be with other disabled people within the mainstream setting. There was a concern that inclusion was not realised through the denial of disability, and a strongly held view that what was necessary was a merge of cultures not a take-over. Several young people also made it clear that they were very happy with the quality of education received in their segregated school, where their needs were recognised and met. They wanted to ensure that the mainstream schools were able to provide the same level of experience. Finally the young people spoke highly of the qualities of many of their special school teachers and were anxious to ensure that these skills and qualities would be internalised by their mainstream teachers.

In general terms much of the research into inclusion has tended to bypass the views and experiences of those who have been excluded. These young people must be able to give their perspective and above all those who are most directly affected by exclusion must be given a role in relation to decisions which directly affect them. Article 12 of the United Nations Convention on the Rights of the Child (1989) asserts that the child has the right to express his or her opinion on all matters affecting him/her. This theme is now high on the educational agenda in Scotland, and the Standards in Scotland's Schools etc. Act (2000) enshrines in law that children have participation rights in relation to school development and education authority plans which impact upon the young person's quality of life. This means that young people with additional support needs should have some say in where they are educated and what the quality of that experience should be like. This may be easier said than done but it is fair to say that there is increasing evidence in Scottish schools and local authorities that we are advancing on this front.

SUMMARY

The presumption of mainstreaming will most certainly impact upon the role of the special school. The Audit Scotland report 'Moving to Mainstream' indicates that the majority of young people with additional support needs are already being educated in mainstream schools and this trend will continue.

However, specialist provision outwith the mainstream will still exist to meet the needs of those who experience more severe/ complex difficulties. As we progress through the twenty-first century there will be fewer special schools catering for a more specific range of needs. These special schools will need to clarify their role within the context of inclusion if they are to emerge as centres of excellence. They will be expected to give high priority to developing collaborative practices with their mainstream partners. These partnerships will be strengthened through reciprocal arrangements whereby skills and expertise are shared. Putting these new systems in place will involve change and there will be barriers to be overcome. The highest priority must be given to listening to the voice of those who have experienced exclusion. They are central to the inclusion debate, and this must not be forgotten.

POINTS FOR REFLECTION

1 The presumption of mainstreaming will pose challenges to special schools. Are special schools always exclusive or do they have a role to play within the context of inclusion?

2 It is increasingly likely that special schools will be linked to mainstream schools in inclusive partnerships. What barriers will need to be overcome to make such partnerships a reality?

3 The impact of exclusion on the lives of people can only be fully understood if we listen to and accept the views of those who have actually experienced it. Are these individuals given real opportunities to have their say and what evidence is there that professionals listen and act upon what they hear?

9 Sustainable inclusion

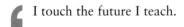

I touch the future I teach.

Christa McAuliffe

Introduction

Change in relation to provision for pupils with additional
support needs has been a continuous process since the watershed
introduced by the seminal reports of 1978 (DES 1978; SED
1978) and the subsequent legislation to support first integration
and currently inclusion. Such changes within education have
created tensions in the profession. Change is dependent on those
affected by it accepting the need for it, feeling that they have
ownership of it and being prepared to drive it forward. Not all
teachers have accepted that challenge, so can inclusion be
sustained?

In terms of the "rights" agenda which underpins the push for
inclusion, education is clearly seen by the UK government as the
catalyst for social change (Blunkett 2002, p. 1). However, we live
in an unequal society where there is poverty and disadvantage.
Investment to raise standards in society must also be targeted at
these very real factors. Education cannot be expected to
overcome these barriers to social equality and social inclusion on
its own. It must be argued that social inclusion is a desirable goal
but it must also be acknowledged that there are key issues that
must be addressed to enable the process of inclusion within our
schools to be fully implemented and maintain momentum. In
this book we have alluded to the stakeholders involved in the
process. This chapter will consider who these stakeholders are
and what issues affect them.

School staff: attitudes and expectations

Staff expectations and attitudes cannot be underestimated in the push towards inclusive schooling. The Scottish Consultative Council on the Curriculum in their document 'Teaching for effective learning' (1990, p. 35) encourages teachers to consider the assumptions that they make about individual learners and on what basis these are made. Such questions are necessary in order to explore teacher and staff attitudes towards inclusion. Expectations and attitudes underpin school ethos and have a powerful influence on pupil experience.

Exploring attitudes is, however, very difficult as they are considered abstract; as Vlachou (1997, p. 37) states, they are 'located in the unconscious and revealed differently in different situations'. Nevertheless it is imperative that teachers and other staff in schools should have positive attitudes towards inclusion thereby promoting the highest expectations for all pupils as the accepted maxim. This will require a radical change in initial teacher education so that future teachers share the vision. Continuing professional development for teachers will also help to raise the quality of teacher awareness in this regard. In the study by Clark (2001) one headteacher of a nursery establishment was very discerning in her recruitment of staff. She always asked what their feelings were towards children with disabilities. This ensured that the issue was aired and attitudinal views were discussed. Appointments to that establishment favoured those with positive attitudes towards disability and inclusion.

Parents, carers and pupils

Partnership with parents and carers is another key issue on the evolutionary route to inclusion. Parental choice must be a possibility. Some parents/carers, in the best interests of their child, may not choose mainstream education. Special education still has a vital role to play for the foreseeable future. Listening to parents and listening to the views, needs and aspirations of pupils is imperative. Parents/carers are, in the main, as concerned about the personal and social aspects of education as they are about the academic aspects. This is discussed by Thomas and O'Hanlon (2000). Those parents/carers who choose mainstream education for their child with additional support needs may be more concerned about their child's acceptance in personal and social domains than with academic performance.

Schools must enter into a dialogue with parents/carers and work towards a partnership with them in the education of their child. In many schools, partnership with parents falls somewhat short of the mark. Partners have equal status and responsibility, and their views and ideas are listened to. A study by Clark, Cooper and Ross-Watt (2004) found that such partnerships were the exception rather than the rule. It must also be acknowledged here that some parents do not seek partnership in their children's education. This reflects an element of society's shortcomings at the present time but where parents/carers are willing to enter into partnership with their children's education this should be wholeheartedly welcomed.

In the same way that listening to parents is important, there is value in listening to the pupils, both those who are being included and those who have no additional support needs. This is also an acknowledgement of pupils' rights. The views of each set are equally important, as pointed out in the work of Allan (1999, p. 118) which refers to mainstream pupils as the 'inclusion gatekeepers'. Just as managers and staff require additional training to facilitate inclusion, pupils can also be supported to examine their self-beliefs, attitudes and expectations. The personal and social education curriculum in schools can be adapted to include issues relating to diversity and inclusion.

Education authorities

Education authorities have a duty to actively ensure that their policies on inclusion are reflected in the practice of schools. Providing guidance and monitoring practice is essential. Self-evaluation for inclusive schools is to be encouraged and the recent guidance 'Inclusive Schooling: Enhancing Policy and Practice' (MacLeod, Frier and Hookey 2003), issued by SEED, will enable schools to evaluate and refine their inclusive practices. Some authorities have, in addition, their own guidance on such self-evaluation.

Education authorities also have a duty to provide support for schools, teachers and pupils to enrich the experience of all concerned. Some of this support will be additional staffing but resources have a part to play as well. The financing of inclusion cannot be underestimated and in this respect authorities are dependent on the generosity of the government. To sustain progression in inclusion the government in Scotland has made a large financial contribution. Nevertheless there appears still to be an unequal distribution of resources across schools, particularly when ICT is considered. Education authorities should perhaps take careful stock of resourcing in their establishments to address the shortfall.

Other professionals

Schools are no longer islands in the sea of local authority provision. Working together with a range of professionals has become the norm in Scottish schools. The new community schools initiative in Scotland was introduced to develop and sustain inter-agency working. When dealing with pupils with additional support needs such collaboration is vital. The agencies involved are education, health and social work, and the combined expertise of this triad can help to complete a rounded picture of a pupil's needs in relation to their educational, physical, emotional, mental and social development.

A good model of inter-agency collaboration has been the Pre-School Community Assessment Team (Pre SCAT) which has successfully utilised a range of professionals and their expertise when making decisions about school and nursery placement and levels of support for children who, in the era of special educational needs, were being considered for a Record of Needs.

Such inter-agency teamwork will also be required to meet the requirement of a Co-ordinated Support Plan. The creation of new community schools has not yet resulted in the expected wholescale collaboration between the agencies involved. Variation in conditions of service, length of day, holidays, employer priorities, etc. creates barriers to such collaboration across professional boundaries. What may help to promote and sustain such collaboration in the future is more investment in multi-disciplinary and inter-agency training as discussed by Campbell, Gillbom, Lunt, Sammons, Warren and Whitby (2002).

School management

Headteachers and senior management must lead by example in inclusive schools. The quality of their leadership in this respect is of paramount importance. These managers cannot be expected to carry the full burden of responsibility for a whole-school response to ensuring equal opportunity and valuing diversity but they must be responsible for fuelling staff enthusiasm to work as a team to support the changes essential to making the vision of inclusion a reality. Participative management on the part of all staff is the key to such collective responsibility, as agreed by Campbell *et al.* (2002) and Nutbrown (1998), but whole-school means more than managers and staff being involved. Pupils, too, should feel that they are a part of the change process and that they have an important role to play to ensure that inclusion continues to progress.

School managers, like all staff, will require professional development. Such professional development is available in the form of the Scottish Qualification for Headship (SQH) which has been well subscribed to in recent years. This course must ensure that it has a specific input on inclusion and additional support needs to guarantee the focus on this at whole-school level. School managers should also be encouraged to involve their support for learning staff in providing staff development for colleagues and in the process of policy formulation in the area of inclusion. Such staff, if they have studied the postgraduate programme in support for learning, have a wealth of knowledge, understanding and skills which can be utilised in this arena.

School staff: training

The training of teachers must now have a focus on inclusion. For some school staff, for example classroom assistants and other support staff, access to training can be a bit more elusive. Such staff, on occasions, appear uncertain about their role in schools and classrooms. Better quality compulsory training must be provided for staff to ensure that they share the vision of inclusion held by their teacher colleagues. Ideally their training and development could be shared with teaching staff so that opportunities for dialogue and discussion are presented and so that each knows about the other's role.

In conclusion

Some of the issues relating to the stakeholders of inclusion have been discussed in this chapter. However, the process towards inclusion must be supported by all of the people already mentioned here, and inclusion is about radical change to the culture that is the school. If short cuts are taken by trying to simply tweak something here or add something there, then the required radical reform necessary to support inclusion will not take place. We must learn from the lessons of the era of integration that the focus must be on, as stated on page 10 of this book, 'requiring schools to think about and remove environmental, structural and attitudinal barriers which underpinned exclusive practice. Inclusion implies systematic change involving radical reform at all levels of the education system'. If we succeed then inclusion in our schools can be sustained, but be prepared for the journey to be long and bumpy.

Reflection

Finally we encourage you, now that you have completed the reading of this book, to reflect on the important issues provided in the summaries of each chapter, and the conclusion above, and to consider the following questions which are essential to your own professional development. Please remember that a good education professional must be prepared to be self-critical and to strive to continue his/her professional development. This type of professional will actively seek to become a truly reflective practitioner who influences change in classrooms and schools and who personally models good practice. A profession which is comprised of such teachers will ensure that inclusion can progress and be sustained. A good inclusive teacher is an effective teacher. We invite you to answer yes or no to the following questions on how inclusive and effective you are.

1 Does the deficit model of labelling continue its existence in your classroom?
2 Are barriers to learning created within the context of your classroom?
3 Do you accept responsibility for the learning of all pupils in your classroom?

4 Do you understand the implications for you as a teacher, of the Disability and Additional Support Needs Legislation?

5 Are pupils in your class fully involved in all activities?

6 Do you understand that inclusion is about all pupils and is wider than those who previously had special educational needs?

7 Do you listen to the views of your pupils?

8 Is partnership with parents valued by you in the support provided for your pupils?

9 Do you provide a differentiated curriculum?

10 Do you value diversity?

11 Are you willing to work collaboratively with colleagues and other agency professionals?

12 Do you treat pupils fairly and equally?

13 Are your pupils encouraged to come to you for help when they are stuck with a task?

14 Do you know which pupils in your class/es have poor self-esteem?

15 Do you seek support from your colleagues?

16 Do you plan work for individuals which targets both their strengths and their needs?

17 When a pupil has a problem with learning do you tend to blame the pupil?

18 Do you give praise for effort?

19 Is personal professional development important to you?

20 Are you committed to inclusion?

21 Do you value the importance of pupils' personal and social development?

22 Are you involved in planning IEPs?

23 Do you feel confident about your ability to support pupils who struggle with learning?

24 Are you familiar with the system of support referral in your school?

25 Do you ensure that pupils are supported in their learning?

Response rating

If your answer to questions 1 and 2 was yes then you need to consider a radical change in your classroom practice.

If you answered yes to question 17 and no to questions 3, 5, 7, 8, 9, 10, 12, 13, 14, 16, 18, 20, 21, 25 you are not modelling inclusive practice and are not fulfilling your duty in line with government and authority policy.

A no to questions 4 and 6 means that you need to research this so that your practice is not in breach of the requirements of the Act and children's rights.

A no response to questions 11, 15, 22 and 24 indicates that you do not work collaboratively.

If you recorded a no against question 19 then you are not modelling true professionalism.

Finally, a no response to question 23 indicates that you require more staff development and support.

If you provided mostly alternative responses to these questions then you are well on the way to becoming a good inclusive effective practitioner with a commitment to professionalism and to the pupils with whom you work.

Only you (and probably your colleagues) know which of these is the real you.

References

Chapter 1

Ainscow, M. (1991). *Effective Schools for All*. London: Fulton.

Allan, J. (1999). *Actively Seeking Inclusion*. London: Falmer Press.

Booth, T. and Ainscow, M. (1998). *From Them to Us – An International Study of Inclusion in Education*. London: Routledge.

Booth, T., and Swann, W. (eds) (1992). *Curriculum for Diversity in Education*. London: Routledge.

DES (Department of Education and Science) (1978). *Special Educational Needs: Report of the Committee of Enquiry into the Education of Handicapped Children and Young People* (The Warnock Report). London: HMSO.

Disability Discrimination Act (1995). London: HMSO.

Dockrell, W., Dunn, W. and Milne, A. (1978). *Special Education in Scotland*. Edinburgh: SCRE.

Education of Defective Children (Scotland) Act (1907).

Education (Disability Strategies and Pupils' Educational Records) (Scotland) Act 2002.

Education (Scotland) Act (1872), (1945), (1974), (1980).

Gilbert, C. and Hart, M. (1990). *Towards Integration*. London: Kogan.

Hamill, P. and Boyd, B. (2000). *Striving for Inclusion*. Glasgow: University of Strathclyde.

Hamill, P. and Boyd, B. (2001). *Inclusive Education: Taking the Initiative*. Glasgow: University of Strathclyde.

Lunacy (Scotland) Act (1862).

Melville Committee Report (1973). *The Training of Staff in Centres for the Mentally Handicapped*. London: DES.

Mittler, P. (2000). *Working Towards Inclusive Education – Social Contexts*. London: Fulton.

Nind, M., Sheehy, K. and Simmons, K. (2003). *Inclusive Education: Learners and Learning Contexts*. London: Fulton.

Pearson, L. and Lindsay, G. (1986). *Special Needs in the Primary School*. London: Nelson.

Sebba, J., Byers, R. and Rose, R. (1995). *Redefining the Whole Curriculum for Pupils with Learning Difficulties*. London: Fulton.

SEED (Scottish Executive Education Department) (2001). *A Teaching Profession for the 21st Century*. Edinburgh: HMSO.

SEED (Scottish Executive Education Department) (2003a). *Moving Forward! Additional Support for Learning*. Edinburgh: HMSO.

SEED (Scottish Executive Education Department) (2003b). *Count Us In – Achieving Inclusion in Scottish Schools*. A Report by HM Inspectors. Edinburgh: HMSO.

Slee, R. (1996). 'Disability, class and poverty: School structures and policing identities', in Christensen, C. and Rizvi, F. (eds) *Disability and the Dilemmas of Education and Justice*. Buckingham: Open University Press.

SOED (Scottish Office Education Department) (1994). *Effective Provision for Special Educational Needs*. Edinburgh: HMSO.

SED (Scottish Education Department) (1978). *The Education of Pupils with Learning Difficulties in Primary and Secondary Schools in Scotland*. Edinburgh: HMSO.

SOEID (Scottish Office Education and Industry Department) (1998). *A Manual of Good Practice in Special Educational Needs*. Edinburgh: HMSO.

Solity, J. (1993). *Special Education*. London: Cassells.

Special Education Treatment (Scotland) Regulations (1954).

The Scottish Parliament (2000) Standards in Scotland's Schools etc. Act. Edinburgh: HMSO.

The Scottish Parliament (2004) Education (Additional Support for Learning) (Scotland) Act, Edinburgh: HMSO.

Thomson, G.O.B. (1983). 'Legislation and provision for the mentally handicapped child in Scotland since 1906'. *Oxford Review of Education*. V9 (3), 233–239.

Thomson, G., Stewart, M. and Ward, K. (1998). *Criteria for Opening a Record of Needs*. Interchange No. 40. Research & Intelligence Unit. Edinburgh: HMSO.

UN (United Nations) (1989). Convention on the Rights of the Child. Articles 2, 23. New York: UN.

Chapter 2

Allan, J. (1999). *Actively Seeking Inclusion*. London: Falmer Press.

Booth, T. and Ainscow, M. (1998). *From Them to Us – An International Study of Inclusion in Education*. London: Routledge.

Buckley, S., Bird, G., Sacks, B. and Archer, T. (2000). 'A comparison of mainstream and special schools education for teenagers with downs syndrome'. *Downs Syndrome Research and Practice* 7 (1).

Children (Scotland) Act 1995.

Clough, P. (ed.) (1998). *Managing Inclusive Education: From Policy to Experience*. London: Chapman.

Corbett, J. (1998). *Special Educational Needs in the Twentieth Century*. London: Chapman.

CSIE (Centre for Studies in Inclusive Education) (1996). *The Inclusive School*. Bristol: CSIE.

Dew-Hughes, D. and Blanford, S. (1998). 'The social development of children with severe learning difficulties'. *Downs Syndrome Research and Practice* 6 (1).

Dew-Hughes, D. (1999). 'Research summary – the social development of children in special schools'. *Downs Syndrome News and Update* 1 (1).

Dyson, A. (1997). 'Social and educational disadvantage: reconnecting special needs education'. *British Journal of Special Education.* 24, (4), 152–157.

Hall, J.T. (1997). *Social Devaluation and Special Education – The Right to Full Mainstream Inclusion*. London: Sage.

Hamill, P. and Boyd, B. (2000). *Striving for Inclusion*. Glasgow: University of Strathclyde.

Hamill, P. and Boyd, B. (2001). *Inclusive Education: Taking the Initiative*. Glasgow: University of Strathclyde.

Hamill, P. and Boyd, B. (2002). *Inclusion: Principles into Practice*. Glasgow: University of Strathclyde.

Hegarty, S. (1991). 'Conclusion' in Ainscow, M. (ed). *Effective Schools for All*. Stafford: NASEN. London: Fulton

Lipsky, D. and Gartner, A. (1996). 'Capable of achievement and worthy of respect'. *Exceptional Children.* 54 (1), 69–74.

Manset, G. and Semmal, M.I. (1997). 'Are inclusive programmes for students with mild disabilities effective?' *Journal of Special Education.* 3, 155–180.

Salend, S. J. and Garrick-Duhaney, L. M. (1999). 'Impact of inclusion on students with and without disabilities and their education'. *Journal of Special Education.* **20**, 114–126.

SCCC (Scottish Consultative Committee on the Curriculum) (1994). *Special Needs Within the 5–14 Curriculum – Support for Learning.* Dundee: SCCC.

Sebba, J. and Ainscow, M. (1996) 'International developments in inclusive schooling: mapping the issues'. *Cambridge Journal of Education.* **26** (1) 5–18.

SEED (Scottish Executive Education Department) (2003a). *Moving Forward! Additional Support for Learning.* Edinburgh: HMSO.

SEED (Scottish Executive Education Department) (2003b). *Count Us In – Achieving Inclusion in Scottish Schools.* A Report by HMI. Edinburgh: HMSO.

SOEID (Scottish Office Education and Industry Department) (1997). *How Good is Our School? Self-evaluation using Performance Indicators.* Edinburgh: HMSO.

Solity, J. (1993). *Special Education.* London: Cassells.

Swann, W. (1988). 'Learning difficulties or curricular reform – integration or differentiation', in Thomas, G. and Feiler, (eds) *Planning for Special Needs: A Whole School Approach.* Oxford: Basil Blackwell.

Thomas, G., Walker, D. and Webb, J. (1998). *The Making of the Inclusive School.* London: Routledge.

Chapter 3

Clark, K. (2001). 'Issues in integrating children with special educational needs at the pre-school stage: a Scottish perspective'. *Journal of Special Needs Education in Ireland* (REACH). **14** (2).

Clark, K., Cooper, M. and Ross-Watt, F. (2004). 'Inclusion: moving beyond the margins'. *Journal of Special Needs Education in Ireland* (REACH). **17** (2).

Cowne, E. (2003). *Developing Inclusive Practice.* London: Fulton.

McNiff, J. (1993). 'Investigating inclusion: a revaluation of a teachers' professional development course', in Wearmouth, J. (ed.) (2001). *Special Educational Provision in the Context of Inclusion.* London: Fulton in association with the Open University.

Roaf, (2001). 'Working with outside agencies' in Wearmouth, J. (ed.) (2001). *Special Educational Provison in the Context of Inclusion.*

London: David Fulton in association with the Open University.

Scottish Executive (2002). *Assessing our Children's Educational Needs: The Way Forward*. Edinburgh: HSMO.

SEED (Scottish Executive Education Department) (2003a). *Moving Forward! Additional Support for Learning*. Edinburgh: HMSO.

SEED (Scottish Executive Education Department) (2003b). *Report of the Consultation on the Draft Additional Support for Learning Bill*. Edinburgh: HMSO.

Scottish Parliament (2003). Education (Additional Support for Learning) (Scotland) Bill, Policy Memorandum. Edinburgh: HMSO.

Scottish Parliament (2004). Education (Additional Support for Learning) (Scotland) Act. Edinburgh: HMSO.

Chapter 4

Armstrong, D. (1996). *Power and Partnership: Children and Special Educational Needs*. London: Routledge.

CACE (1967). *Children and their Primary Schools*. Plowden Report. London: HMSO.

Enquire, (1999). 'A Parents' Guide to Special Educational Needs – Enquire'.

Galton, M., Simon, B. and Croll, P. (1988). *Inside the Primary Classroom*. London: Routledge & Kegan Paul.

Hamill, P. and Boyd, B. (2001). 'Rhetoric or reality: inter-agency provision for young people with challenging behaviour'. *Journal of Social, Emotional and Behavioural Difficulties*. 6 (3), 135–149.

Hamill, P. and Boyd, B. (2003). 'Interviews with young people about behavioural support: equality, fairness and rights', in Nind, M., Sheehy, K. and Simmons, K. (eds), *Inclusive Education: Learners and Learning Contexts*. London: Fulton.

Lacey, P. (2001). *Support Partnerships: Collaboration in Action*. London: Fulton.

O'Brien, T. and Guiney, D. (2001). *Differentiation in Teaching and Learning: Principles and Practice*. London: Continuum.

SED (Scottish Office Education Department) (1978). *The Education of Pupils with Learning Difficulties in Primary and Secondary Schools in Scotland*. Edinburgh: HMSO.

SEED (Scottish Executive Education Department) (2001). *Better Behaviour – Better Learning*. Edinburgh: HMSO.

SEED (Scottish Executive Education Department) (2001). *Improving Our Schools – Assessing Children's Educational Needs – The Way Forward?* Edinburgh: HMSO.

SEED (Scottish Executive Education Department) (2003a). *Moving Forward! Additional Support for Learning.* Edinburgh: HMSO.

SEED (Scottish Executive Education Department) (2003b). *Count Us In – Achieving Inclusion in Scottish Schools.* Edinburgh: HMSO.

SOED (Scottish Office Education Department) (1995). *Standards and Quality in Scottish Schools 1992–95.* Edinburgh: HMSO.

SOED (Scottish Office Education Department) (1998). *Raising Standards in Schools – Setting Targets.* Edinburgh: HMSO.

SOEID (Scottish Office Education and Industry Department) (1994a). *Support for Learning – SEN within the 5–14 Programme.* Edinburgh: HMSO.

SOEID (Scottish Office Education and Industry Department) (1994b). *Effective Provision for Special Educational Needs.* Edinburgh: HMSO.

SOEID (Scottish Office Education and Industry Department) (1996). *Achievement for All.* Edinburgh: HMSO.

SOEID (Scottish Office Education and Industry Department) (1997). *How Good is Our School? Self-evaluation using Performance Indicators.* Edinburgh: HMSO.

SOEID (Scottish Office Education and Industry Department) (1997). *Raising the Standard: a White Paper on Education and Skills Development in Scotland.* Edinburgh: HMSO.

SOEID (Scottish Office Education and Industry Department) (1998). *A Manual of Good Practice in Special Educational Needs.* Edinburgh: HMSO.

SOEID (Scottish Office Education and Industry Department) (1999). *New Community Schools – The Prospectus.* Edinburgh: HMSO.

UN (United Nations) (1989). Convention on the Rights of the Child. Articles 2, 23. New York: UN.

Chapter 5

Ball, C. (1994). *Start Right: The Importance of Early Learning.* London: Royal Society of Arts.

Bruner, J.S. (1983). *Child's talk: learning to use language.* Oxford: Oxford University Press.

Barrs, M. (1990). *Patterns of Learning, Primary Language Record and the National Curriculum*. London: Centre for Language in Primary Education.

DES (Department of Education and Science) (1978). *Special Educational Needs: Report of the Committee of Enquiry into the Education of Handicapped Children and Young People* (The Warnock Report). London: HMSO.

Scottish Executive (2001). *For Scotland's Children*. Edinburgh: HMSO.

SEED (Scottish Executive Education Department) (2003). *Moving Forward! Additional Support for Learning*. Edinburgh: HMSO.

SEED (Scottish Executive Education Department) (2000). *The Structure and Balance of the Curriculum*. Dundee: Learning and Teaching Scotland.

SEED (Scottish Executive Education Department) (2002). *National Priorities in Education: Support Pack for Primary Schools*. Edinburgh: HMSO.

SEED (Scottish Executive Education Department) (2003). *Moving Forward: Additional Support for Learning*. Edinburgh: HMSO.

SOED (Scottish Office Education Department) (1994a) *Education of Children under 5 in Scotland*. Edinburgh: HMSO.

SOED (Scottish Office Education Department) (1994b) *Effective Provision for Special Educational Needs*. Edinburgh: HMSO.

SOEID (Scottish Office Education and Industry Department) (1997). *A Curriculum Framework for Children in their Pre-school Year*. Edinburgh: HMSO.

SOEID (Scottish Office Education and Industry Department) (1998). *A Manual of Good Practice in Special Educational Needs*. Edinburgh: HMSO.

SOEID (Scottish Office Education and Industry Department) (1999). *The 3–5 Curriculum Guidelines*. Edinburgh: HMSO.

Sylva, K., Roy, C. and Painter, M. (1980). *Childwatching at Playgroup and Nursery school*. London: Grant McIntyre.

Vygotsky, L.S. (1962). *Thought and Language*. Cambridge, MA MIT Press.

Chapter 6

Fidge, L. (1994). *Rol 'n write handwriting activity worksheets and rol 'n write alphabet*. Wisbech: LDA.

Portwood, M. (2000). *Understanding Developmental Dyspraxia*. London: Fulton.

SOED (Scottish Office Education Department) (1978). *The Education of Pupils with Learning Difficulties in Primary and Secondary Schools in Scotland*. Edinburgh: HMSO.

SOED (Scottish Office Education Department) (1994). *Effective Provision for Special Educational Needs*. Edinburgh: HMSO.

SOED (Scottish Office Education Department) (1995). *Support for Learning within the 5–14 Curriculum*. Edinburgh: HMSO.

SOEID (Scottish Office Education and Industry Department) (1998a). *A Manual of Good Practice in Special Educational Needs*. Edinburgh: HMSO.

SOEID (Scottish Office Education and Industry Department) (1998b) *Parents as Partners: Enhancing the Role of Parents in School Education* (a Discussion Paper). Edinburgh: HMSO.

Teodorescu, I. and Addy, L.M. (1996). *The Teodorescu Perceptuo-motor Programme. Write from the Start*. Wisbech: LDA.

The Scottish Parliament (2004). Additional support for learning (Scotland) Act. Edinburgh: HMSO.

Chapter 7

Boyd, B. and Simpson, M. (2003). 'Primary–Secondary Liaison in Scottish Education'. Second Edition, Post-Devolution in Bryce, T.G.K. and Humes, W.M. (eds). Edinburgh: Edinburgh University Press.

CCC (Consultative Committee on the Curriculum) (1986). Education 10–14 in Scotland. Dundee: Information and Publication Services (CCC).

Cooper, P. (1993) *Effective Schools for Disaffected Students: Integration and Segregation*. London: Routledge.

Hamill, P. and Boyd, B. (2000). *Striving for Inclusion*. Glasgow: University of Strathclyde.

Hamill, P. and Boyd, B. (2001) *Inclusive Education: Taking the Initiative*. Glasgow: University of Strathclyde.

Hamill, P. and Boyd, B. (2002) *Inclusion: Principles into Practice*. Glasgow: University of Strathclyde.

Lennon, F. (2003) 'Organisation and management in the secondary school in Scottish education'. In Bryce, T.G.K. and Humes, W.M. (eds). Edinburgh: Edinburgh University Press.

O'Brien, T. (1998). *Promoting Positive Behaviour*. London: Hodder & Stoughton.

Porter, L. (2000). *Behaviour in Schools – Theory and Practice for Teachers*. Buckingham: Open University Press.

SEED (Scottish Executive Education Department) (2001). *Better Behaviour – Better Learning*. Edinburgh: HMSO.

SEED (Scottish Executive Education Department) (2003). *Count Us In – Achieving Inclusion in Scottish Schools*. Edinburgh: HMSO.

SED (Scottish Education Department) (1978). *The Education of Pupils with Learning Difficulties in Primary and Secondary Schools in Scotland*. Edinburgh: HMSO.

SOED (Scottish Office Education Department) (1994a). *Effective Provision for Special Educational Needs*. Edinburgh: HMSO.

SOEID (Scottish Office Education and Industry Department) (1994b). *Special Needs within the 5–14 Curriculum*. Edinburgh: HMSO.

SOEID (Scottish Office Education and Industry Department) (1998). *A Manual of Good Practice in Special Educational Needs*. Edinburgh: HMSO.

SOEID (Scottish Office Education and Industry Department) (1999). *New Community Schools: The Prospectus*. Edinburgh: HMSO.

Susskind, L. (1989). *Breaking the Impasse: Consensual Approaches to Resolving Public Disputes*. USA: Basic Books.

Chapter 8

Audit Scotland (2003). *Moving to Mainstream – The Inclusion of Pupils with Special Educational Needs in Mainstream Schools*. Prepared in partnership with HMIE.

Cheminais, R. (2003). *Closing the Inclusion Gap – Special and Mainstream Schools Working in Partnership*. London: Fulton.

Corbett, J. (2001). *Supporting Inclusive Education – A Connective Pedagogy*. London: Routledge.

Cook, T., Swain, J. and French, S. (2003). 'Voices from segregated schooling: towards an inclusive education system'. In Nind, M., Sheehy, K. and Simmons, K. (eds), *Inclusive Education: Learners and Learning Contexts*. London: Fulton, pp.103–120.

DFES (2001). Inclusive Schooling: *Children with Special Educational Needs*. London: Department for Education and Skills.

Dyson, A. and Gains, C. (eds) (1993). *Rethinking Special Needs in Mainstream Schools: Towards the Year 2000*. London: Fulton.

Dyson, A. (1997). 'Social and educational disadvantage: reconnecting special needs education'. *British Journal of Special Education.* **24**(4), 152–7.

Evans, J. and Lunt, I. (1994). *Collaborating for Effectiveness.* Buckingham: Open University Press.

Farrell, P. (1996). 'Integration: where do we go from here?' In Coupe O'Kane, J. and Goldbort, J. (eds), *Whose Choice?* London: Fulton.

Fletcher-Campbell, F. and Kington, A. (2000). 'Links between special schools and mainstream schools: a follow up survey'. *Journal in Research in Special Educational Needs.* **1** (3).

Hall, J. (1996). 'Integration, inclusion: what does it all mean?' In Coupe O'Kane, J. and J. Goldbort (eds), *Whose Choice?* London: Fulton.

Hegarty, S. (1994). *Response in Planning and Diversity: Special Schools and their alternatives.* Stafford: NASEN.

SEED (Scottish Executive Education Department) (2003). *Moving Forward! Additional Support for Learning.* Edinburgh: HMSO.

The Scottish Parliament (2000). Standards in Scotland's Schools etc. Act. Edinburgh: HMSO.

Tomlinson, S. (1982). *A Sociology of Special Education.* London: Routledge & Kegan Paul.

Chapter 9

Allan, J. (1999). *Actively Seeking Inclusion and Pupils with Special Needs in Mainstream Schools.* London: Falmer Press.

Blunkett, D. (2000). *Raising Aspirations in the 21st Century.* London: DfEE.

Campbell, C., Gillbom, D., Lunt, J., Sammons, P., Vincent, C., Warren, S. and Whitby, G. (2003). 'Strategies and issues for inclusive schooling', in Campbell, G. (ed.), *Developing Inclusive Schooling: Perspectives, Policies and Practices.* London: Institute of Education, University of London.

Clark, K. (2001). 'Issues in integrating children with special educational needs at the pre-school stage: a Scottish Perspective'. *Journal of Special Needs Education in Ireland* (REACH). **14**, (2).

Clark, K., (2004). 'Inclusion: moving beyond the margins'. *Journal of Special Needs Education in Ireland* (REACH). **17**, (2).

DES (Department for Education and Science) (1978). *Special Educational Needs: Report of the Committee of Enquiry into the Education of Handicapped Children and Young People* (The Warnock Report). London: HMSO.

MacLeod, D., Frier, F. and Hookey, B. (2003). *Inclusive Schooling: Enhancing Policy and Practice*. Edinburgh: SEED.

Nutbrown, C. (1998). 'Managing to include? Rights, responsibilities and respect', in Clough, P. (ed.). *Managing Inclusive Education: from Policy to Experience*. London: Chapman.

Scottish Consultative Council on the Curriculum (1990). *Teaching for Effective Learning*. Dundee: SCCC.

SED (Scottish Education Department) (1978). *The Education of Pupils with Learning Difficulties in Primary and Secondary Schools in Scotland*. Edinburgh: HMSO.

Thomas, G., O'Hanlon, C. (eds) (2000). *Inclusive Education*. London: McGraw-Hill.

Vlachou, A.D. (1997). *Struggles for Inclusive Education*. Buckingham: Open University Press.

Index